Frontispiece
Construction in slab glass, steel
and resin, by the author.

GLASS, RESIN AND METAL CONSTRUCTION

Peter Tysoe

MILLS & BOON LIMITED LONDON

First published in England, 1971,
by Mills & Boon Limited,
17–19 Foley Street,
London W1A 1DR

ⓒ Peter Tysoe 1971

ISBN 0.263.51394.7

Made and printed in
Great Britain by
W. S. Cowell Ltd at the
Butter Market, Ipswich, Suffolk.

LIST OF CONTENTS

ACKNOWLEDGEMENTS

The author would like to thank all those who have helped him by permitting the reproduction of photographs (acknowledged in their places in the book) and by giving advice which, in the case of fellow-craftsmen, has included a generous willingness to disclose details of their own methods of working.

Special mention must be made of: Ray Bradley; Lawrence Lee; Keith New; John Tiranti; and members of the firms of CIBA and Scott Bader, who read the text.

Plate 1
Slab glasses. Each slab is
8" × 12" × 1".

BIBLIOGRAPHY

ARMITAGE, E. L. Stained Glass: History, Craft and
   Modern Use. 1959. Leonard Hill.
BAKER, J. and LAMMER, A. English Stained Glass.
   1960. Thames & Hudson.
CLARKE, P. J. Plastics for Schools.
   1970. Allman & Son.
LEE, L. Stained Glass. Handbooks for Artists series.
   1967. Oxford University Press.
PIPER, J. Stained Glass: Art or Anti-Art? 1971.
   Studio Vista.
REYNTIENS, P. The Technique of Stained Glass.
   1967. Batsford.
SOWERS, R. Stained Glass. An Architectural Art.
   1965. Zwemmer.
WOODFORDE, C. English Stained & Painted Glass.
   1954. Oxford University Press.

INTRODUCTION

This book is based on the practical experience gained by the author, a sculptor, who has been working in glass for eight years and has been developing his own approach to broader techniques in glass which have become possible with the availability of new resins developed for industrial applications. The information given is based on the practical applications, developed in his studio which is engaged in the full-time production of murals and sculpture for architects, designers and private clients. Not only the advantages, but the practical problems of the different techniques (including certain hazards and the appropriate safety precautions) are fully explained. Illustrated stage-by-stage examples of the techniques are given with descriptions of materials used, and the equipment needed for setting up a working area.

No theory of design as such has been advanced, but it is hoped that the examples shown in the book will help readers to form their own views of the kind of design that works well in these materials.

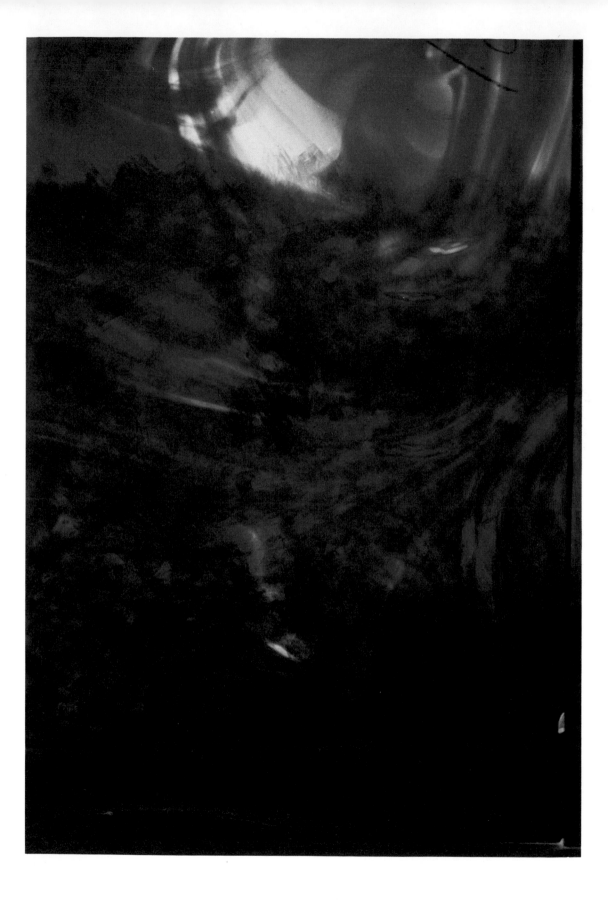

1
GLASS

Plate 2
Single sheet of antique glass.
Approximately 4' high.

In defining 'glass' as used in the context of this book it will be seen from the illustrations of the work produced that there has been a completely new approach to the medium. From the traditional leaded antique glass ('stained glass') the production of thicker slab glasses together with the development of polyester and epoxy resins have led the way to freeing the medium and making possible the formation of panels, constructions and free glass sculpture. The development of coloured slabs of glass, approximately 1" thick, 12" long × 8" wide (known as 'Dalles de Verre' in France, where they were first made before the war), led to their use as cut pieces, set into concrete panels, which could be used to make large wall areas in churches and other buildings. The concrete could give larger masses of dark area in contrast to the brilliant thickness of the coloured glasses; the concrete being the approximate equivalent of the leading in a traditional 'stained glass' window. Several artists saw the potential of the slabs, used rather more freely to show the edge qualities of the glasses, and began work using various opaque and transparent synthetic bonding adhesives to create exciting forms and wall panels where no dark intermediate areas were required.

The thick slabs have a depth and three-dimensional quality which, combined with synthetic adhesives, readily lend themselves to development into two- and three-dimensional forms. It is a misnomer to call any of these more recent developments, including slab glasses and concrete, 'stained glass' and the term should not be used in this context. 'Coloured glass', 'glass constructions' or 'glass sculpture' are terms that accurately describe these developments, which are more frequently being used by people who have rarely, if ever, worked in the traditional leaded glass techniques; although the thinner antique coloured glasses, which are painted with opaque colours and fired in a kiln to produce painted pieces ready for leading up into 'stained glass', can be used in their own right in glass in resin elements. The variegated textures and colours in these glasses can be very beautiful. Those produced by Hartley Wood & Co. in Northumberland, England, have great character, with wavy and streaky surfaces in addition to variations in tone and colouring in individual sheets. These are available up to 24″ × 15″ in size with the thicknesses varying between $\frac{1}{10}$″ and $\frac{3}{16}$″ and can be used alone, or combined with the 1″ thick slabs.

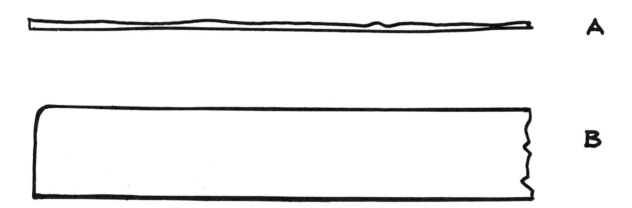

A

B

Antiques are supplied in clear, pale tinted and richly coloured sheets. Variations in the glass are caused by the method of production. The flat sheets are obtained by dipping a glass-blower's tube into molten glass to collect a globule of the glass on the end. The glass worker then blows the globule into a bubble which is gradually formed into a long cylindrical shape with a rounded end. The ends are trimmed and the cylinder is split by running a cold edge down its length while the glass is still plastic, when it falls flat into sheet form. The irregularities on the surface of the glass result from this handmade process and give the glass its interesting variations in

Figure 1
A Typical cross-section through antique sheet, actual size.
B Typical cross-section through slab glass, actual size.

surface and colour. Some colours, red in particular, are 'flashed' onto the surface of a cylinder of clear glass by dipping the molten clear glass globule into another colour, which covers the surface as the form is blown. Flashed glass can be easily recognized when the piece is held edge on and the colour of the body of the glass can be seen with the thin surface layer on top. The surface layer is sometimes etched away to expose the clear, or base coloured glass, to achieve textures, patterns or designs. This is a

Plates 3 and 4
Two more views of antique sheet glass.

Plate 5 (overleaf, top)
Glass Appliqué screens to Bar and Restaurant, Post House Hotel, Hampstead, designed and produced by Ray Bradley.
The hotel was built on the site of the home of the Vandervell family, who developed the Vanwall Formula 1 car, and this has inspired the theme of simple but dominant forms derived from an aerial viewpoint of racing circuits. Use has been made of glass mosaic, plate glass and textured glass, with a transparent epoxy resin.
By courtesy of Ray Bradley.

recognized technique in leaded glass panels, which could also be utilized in glass and resin work. (A good textbook on stained glass will give the techniques and materials involved in this process.)

Where coloured antique glasses are needed without very marked surface undulations, for bonding purposes, some glasses produced by the St-Just-sur-Loire factory of the St Gobain Company in France may be useful. These are imported into this country — the agents being given in the Appendix. Generally, these glasses are more even in thickness and are flatter. They still have interesting variations with enclosed bubbled effects on a smaller scale than most of those found in the English antiques, and it is useful to build up a selection of both types of glass for varying applications.

Commercial plate, wired and textured glasses are readily available from glass merchants and can be used in combination with antique coloured glasses. Mirrored glass is also easily obtained and can sometimes be effectively bonded in panels with clear and coloured glasses.

Slab glasses, mentioned previously, are produced by casting molten glass in 12″ × 8″ moulds and vary in thickness; generally from $\frac{7}{8}$″ to 1″. The bottom surface picks up the slight irregularities of the mould surface, while the top is smooth. Irregularities and air bubbles give each slab an individual character. Colours are made in practically every tint, from white to very dark tones. While, in theory, any colour could be matched in colour and intensity, the supply will generally be restricted to the range available at the stockists. Where smaller individual work is concerned, it is usual to be able to select from a fair range held by the suppliers, but if very large numbers are required it is wise to check on supplies, bearing in mind that the colours are produced by the 'pot'. The

Plates 6 and 6(a)
(page 14, below; page 15)
Set of glass and resin panels designed and executed by the author for the Viking Hotel, York, with a detail from one of them. (Architects: Fitzroy Robinson and Partners. Interior design by Brian Tarrant.)

pot will usually cast approximately 80 slabs in one colour tint and when the next pot is made in the same colour, there is likely to be some variation. If a large number of slabs were needed in the same colour and tone, or you wanted to re-order the same colour as slabs in stock or already used, some difficulty might be found in matching them exactly. In the case of matching to glass previously used it is helpful to send a sample of the glass already held when ordering, so as to be sure that the colour and tone of the glass from the new batch is acceptable. The fact that the previous batch has been numbered the same does not necessarily mean that it will not vary in colour. These variations can be annoying if you are caught out unawares in the middle of a large job by changes in the material. Careful planning is required, especially when thinking of the glass needed for larger commissions.

As the glass slabs are cut and chipped, as described in a later section, various small pieces will be accumulated. These pieces will vary from quite large lumps down to very small chippings, which can be stored and sorted into various sizes for use as packing in the resin areas around the larger slab pieces when used as panels. Besides contrasting with the slab areas these small pieces of glass set in the resin have the added advantage of reducing the contraction rate which is found in larger areas of cast resin. These small pieces can be used on their own with resin to form more intricate and detailed designs and should therefore always be stored safely and kept in the studio. Wherever possible, sorting the chips into various colours and storing them in separate containers is always worthwhile.

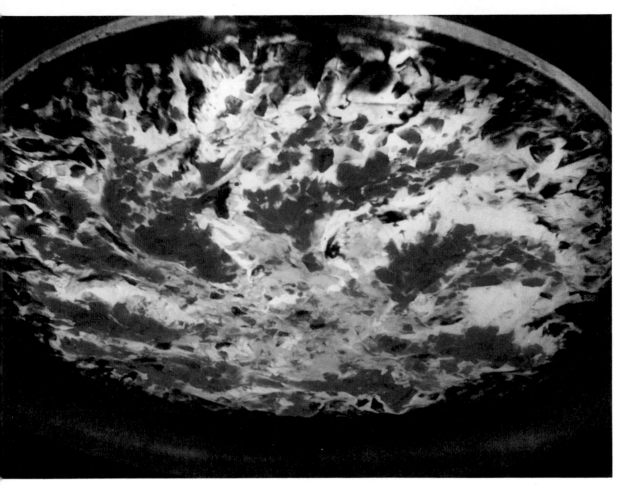

Plate 8
*'Fireball' — ceiling panel designed
and executed by the author for the
National Coal Board, for a stand at
the Ideal Home Exhibition. Mainly
of glass fibre with small glass
pieces embedded — consequently
light in weight.*

Plate 7 (above, opposite)
*Slab glass construction with epoxy
resin, mounted on welded steel,
by the author. Collection of the
City Art Gallery, Plymouth.*

Plate 7(a) (below, opposite)
A detail of the same construction.

2
RESINS

The two resins used in most of the work described in this book, are polyester and epoxy. They are both technically known as 'thermosetting'. Strictly, the word resin is only applicable to the liquid basic material, as when it is changed from liquid to solid state by the addition of catalyst and accelerators, the liquid resin is converted by chemical reaction into a rigid material. Thermosetting plastics undergo a chemical change when the catalyst (hardener) is added and once the process is completed, the plastics cannot be changed back into the previous liquid state by the application of heat, unlike 'thermoplastics' (acrylic, celluloid, polystyrene, pvc, nylon and polyethylene), which can generally be heated and cooled in a mould to achieve the required shape. If heat is re-applied to a thermoplastic it can revert to its previous shape.

Acrylic (methyl methacrylate), well known as 'Perspex' or 'Plexiglas' clear or coloured material, is also available as resin or syrup. It has been given a short section at the end of this chapter and in the Material Suppliers Appendix.

Polyesters have been developed since 1942; the epoxies since 1947. The name polyester is derived from organic chemistry, where the reaction between an acid and an alcohol produces an ester, e.g. acid + alcohol = ester + water. By using a special type of alcohol, this reaction can produce a polyester (Greek poly-, many). With the removal of the water and the addition of other chemicals, the various types of the resin are produced.

A good handbook, produced by the larger manufacturers of the resin, will give a detailed account of the process, including the molecular structure of the resin, before and after polymerization, which is the term used for the transformation process started by the addition of the catalyst and accelerator.

There are many varying types of both polyester and epoxy resin produced, for specific applications, and it is necessary to make sure that the type bought is right for the application for which it is required. The majority of polyester resins are produced for use in the making up of glass reinforced plastics (GRP or RP), for use in boatbuilding, coachbuilding and building industries, etc. As the resin in itself does not have enough mechanical strength to be used alone in these applications, it is combined with glassfibre (usually in mat or cloth form), which, when saturated and made rigid with the hardened resin, makes forms with great strength. A resin used in boatbuilding may be filled with pigment and may not need to be clear, but a specialized casting resin may have been formulated to give the maximum amount of clarity possible. To achieve this, some of the physical strength may have to be sacrificed, but this will not matter as the application of the clear resin will generally not require the physical properties of a boatbuilding resin. It is therefore important that the correct resin is used for the purpose for which it is intended and if in any doubt, the manufacturer should be contacted and his advice obtained. Generally, the manufacturers are very helpful in giving advice and they have research laboratories constantly working on new products and applications. However, it will be found that their recommendations will be based on ideal temperatures and draught-free conditions which it may not always be possible to attain. Some of the practical problems which arise in the studio/workshop are dealt with in later sections.

Both polyester and epoxy are easy to handle and need only simple equipment, but they have varying characteristics. An important difference is that of cost, as epoxy resin is at least four times as expensive as polyester. The basic qualities of the two materials are as follows:

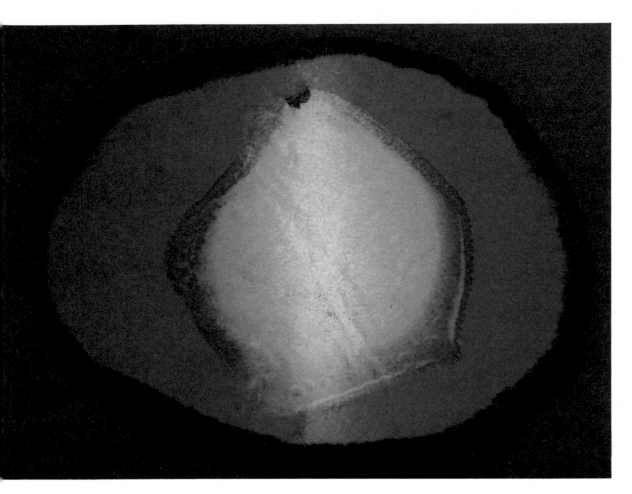

Plate 9 (*left*)
*Display box internally illuminated,
with a laminated glass fibre panel
using opaque and translucent
pigmented polyester resin, approx.
$\frac{1}{8}$" thick.*

Plate 10 (*above*)
A detail of the same panel.

POLYESTER RESIN

Supplied in a liquid state in various viscosities.
Clearer varieties, known as 'water white' or 'water
clear' in manufacturers' lists, are used for translucent
work and in combination with glass. The term 'water
white' is slightly misleading, as none of this resin is as
transparent as acrylic (perspex) or water white
epoxy, but it appears to be clearer in thin sections
and its very slight straw colour in thicker sections is
usually acceptable. If this tint is not wanted, the
addition of a slight amount of translucent blue
polyester pigment will kill it. In fact it turns the base
colour into a very light greyish colour, which gives a
much clearer effect. The resin is transformed into a
rigid material by the addition of the hardener —
sometimes known as the catalyst. Alone, the catalyst
would take a considerable time to harden the resin
and would leave the surface sticky. The time would
depend on the temperature that the material is
subjected to, but it could be a week or so. To

Plate 11
Top row, left to right: polythene catalyst dispenser with gradations marked in mls (cc;) 1 lb tin of polyester resin; polythene dispenser for accelerator, also graduated. Bottom row: laminating brush; finned roller; mohair roller for depositing resin into glass fibre mat.

overcome this, an accelerator, or promotor, is used which, depending on the amount added, can shorten the polymerization or hardening process to under an hour. Catalysts are usually an organic peroxide, supplied in liquid or paste form; accelerators are generally a cobalt soap dispersion and supplied in liquid state. When used in 'normal' glass fibre applications, catalysts are used in a 1% or 2% proportion, by volume, to the amount of resin used. Accelerator is used in a 1% to 4% amount to the base resin. As a general rule, the amount of catalyst should remain constant, while the hardening rate should be adjusted by varying the proportion of accelerator.

WARNING. Catalyst and accelerator must never be mixed directly together. They must be added to the resin separately. If mixed directly together they react explosively. Catalyst, being an organic peroxide, must be handled with care to avoid contact with skin and eyes. Wash immediately with water if it does splash onto the hands. Contact with cellulosic materials should be avoided – spontaneous combustion could result.

The amount of accelerator used will be determined by the working temperature. An average working temperature is 68°F (20°C). If the temperature falls below 59°F (15°C) trouble can result, possibly from undercure, and tacky surfaces usually ensue from work done at low temperatures, or in draughty conditions. Some resins can be supplied with accelerators already added, but more usually the accelerator is added by the consumer.

An advantage with polyester is that clear varieties can be obtained with a fire-retardant additive already mixed into the resin. This is of use in work which is required for public buildings and exhibitions. Clear resins can usually be obtained in at least two varying viscosities, i.e. in a water-like consistency or in a slightly thicker mix.

Figure 2(a)
Massed quantity of resin will gel and overheat if the 'normal' amount of catalyst and accelerator is added.

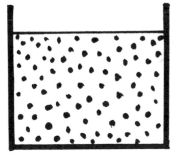

Figure 2(b)
Dispersed resin will not gel so quickly.

While manufacturers' handbooks are extremely useful, it must be appreciated that they are mainly designed for commercial GRP uses, where the resin is dispersed in thinner laminates spread over larger areas. When a resin is catalysed and accelerator is added in a normal temperature the polymerization or

Plate 12
Head of Janus, by the author.
Translucent polyester resin
coloured with amber pigment.

hardening process creates a certain amount of heat in the laminate. When the thickness is no more than $\frac{1}{8}$" the heat build-up (known as 'exotherm') is well dispersed and will have no harmful effect. But when a casting is formed, from the same amount of material, but massed together, so that it is in volume with some thickness, the heat will be marked and the casting will become extremely hot. Smoke can be generated and the casting may crack (the temperature of an unfilled casting can rise to over 300°F (150°C) and discolouration will take place. To overcome this extreme exotherm, the 'normal' amounts of accelerator may have to be reduced and in some conditions, i.e. very hot weather, the amount of catalyst as well, or the thickness of the casting will have to be made up by pouring the resin in several thinner layers, allowing sufficient time for the heat to disperse between each operation.

Associated with this heat problem is the fact that polyester, unfilled with any other material, contracts up to 8% in volume, unlike epoxy, which shrinks very little. This is a problem where glass is to be embedded, as this shrinkage could cause cracking, if poured at one time, but it is solved by the modification of the base resin with a flexible polyester.

Polyester is not suitable for long-term adhesion of thin glasses (glass appliqué). It tends to peel away in thin sections. Epoxy is usually satisfactory for this job.

It should be emphasized that, while general guidelines can be laid down, the flexibility in use of this resin makes it imperative that tests are carried out with measured amounts of the materials involved before larger scale work is started. Methods of measuring catalysts and accelerator are given in the equipment section. Unless recorded tests are undertaken it will be found that results will vary considerably. The important factor of the working temperature should be taken into account.

The polymerization process can be broken down into three stages:
1. Gel time – the period from the mixing of the catalysed resin with the accelerator to the setting of the resin to a soft gel.
2. Hardening time – from setting of the resin to the time when it is hard enough for a moulding or laminate to be taken out of a mould or former.
3. Maturing time – hours, days or even weeks later, when the moulding or laminate has acquired its full hardness and stability. While a hardened casting can be taken out from a mould, its final form will not be achieved until it has matured. During this period contractions can take place which can lead to warping, especially in castings and laminates of uneven thickness. A matured cast will not be subject to further warping.

Polyester can be poured and cast into moulds made of wood, plaster, GRP or silicon or vinyl 'rubbers'. Porous materials, like wood or plaster, should be sealed with a solution of shellac or cellulose acetate. A releasing agent is needed to stop the resin adhering to these materials and GRP moulds, which are made with the same resin. Silicone-free wax polish, buffed or polished to give a shiny surface, and polyvinyl alcohol (PVAL) applied in a thin film which dries to form a fine skin, are both used for this purpose. Silicone wax polishes can increase the surface tension of resins, causing the condition known as 'fish eye'. A porous material, e.g. plaster, will need sealing, waxing and a PVAL application for the first casts. Once the surface is well sealed subsequent casts from the mould will only need the thin PVAL coating, applied evenly with brush or sponge.

The 'rubber' moulding materials – vinyl, a 'hot melt'

material, which can be re-melted and used again and again, or silicone rubber, a 'cold cast' two-part material which is mixed like a resin and can only be used once — need no releasing agents.

Polythene and cellulose sheetings (cellophane) are incompatible with resins and have excellent releasing qualities. While this book is not specifically written for the application of plastics used on their own, the above points are touched on, as an elementary background is necessary for the user of these materials. Again, a good handbook from a resin manufacturer will be found to be invaluable for anyone using his products.

Acetone, or a standard resin solvent, will clean and remove ungelled resin from tools and brushes, but once the material has hardened, any brushes will be unusable if not cleaned and metal mixing spatulas, etc. will have to be chipped or burnt off to remove solid material.

When resin containers are unsealed, the very distinct odour of polyester will be noticed. While this is not harmful in the uncatalysed or catalysed state, good ventilation is needed to disperse the fumes which accompany larger areas of the material.

Barrier and hand-cleaning creams are advisable, together with protective, or very old clothing and shoes. Once resin particles are dropped onto anything cleaning off becomes very difficult, especially with catalysed material.

The storage, or 'shelf life' of polyester varies with the temperature to which it is subjected. It is given an average life of six months to one year by the makers, if stored at temperatures not exceeding 68°F (20°C), but I have used resin two years old which has worked quite well. At this age, though, the results can be

Plate 14(a)
'Sunburst' — lighted panel, approx.
5' × 2' 6", made on a curved
hardboard former with resins being
built up gradually around the
pieces of glass.

Plate 14(b)
The panel shown in its setting. It is
suspended from the wall by a
metal back frame.

Plate 13
Glass and resin twin lighting units
by the author, with back lighting.
Each unit, in slab glasses, resins
and glass-fibre, is 18" × 18".

unpredictable. Supplies should be stored in a cool, dry place, away from any heating appliances.

Both opaque and translucent pigments are readily available from stockists. The translucent colours are usually dispersed in resin ready for mixing into the clear resin and are effective in tinting or richly colouring the base resin, while keeping the translucency of the material. These will be found to be of most use with glass panels and constructions, but opaque, non-transparent pigments can be used to give areas of solid colour if required. If opaque colours are required to show no light through at all when displayed against light, a filler powder (mica, or other material specified and obtainable from stockists) is mixed in with the coloured resin to thicken the mix. Where filler powders are used the amount of catalyst may have to be increased to compensate for this. An obvious use of opaque, filled resin is in the use of dark coloured areas, e.g. black, to give contrasting, or drawn, areas against the clear or coloured transparent glasses and resins.

In use, the pigment supplied in resin will be found to mix more easily if it is added to an equal amount of clear resin and stirred well until it becomes an even, lump-free dispersion. This will then be able to be mixed into the base resin without the small lumps which can be present and give uneven colouring in the completed laminate or casting. Pigments tend to become lumpy if the container tins are left open to the air when not being used.

Polyester, when used as a 'cold cast' technique, which is the technical term for laminating and casting where the materials are mixed and applied without the use of industrial hot presses, is a versatile material. It is easily mixed and used, but because it is so versatile it does need patience and experiment to gain a full working knowledge of the material. The advantages, together with the low cost, make it a very useful material for the studio. Any problems, which particularly occur when casting thicker sections, can be overcome once a working knowledge is gained and this will only be achieved by using the material. The importance of making small samples and recording the working temperature, amounts of resin, catalyst and accelerator used, cannot be over-emphasized.

Each application will call for its own particular solution, but the following general guide is given for resin/catalyst/accelerator mixes. It should be noted that:
(a) Catalyst mixes can be supplied in varying strengths — usually 1% or 2% mixtures.
(b) Not all cobalt accelerators are supplied in the same concentrations. There are 1% and 6% cobalt solutions; accelerator E, supplied by Scott Bader, is approximately 4%.

Thin panels and laminates with glass fibre — up to approximately $\frac{1}{8}''$ thickness.
To 1 lb resin weight.
Catalyst/hardener (check to see if supplied as a 1% or a 2% strength mixture).
  1% mixture — add 8 ml (cc) to 1 lb resin.
  2% mixture — add 4 ml (cc) to 1 lb resin.
(Check suppliers instructions on use, storage, etc.)

Accelerator: Add from 1% to 4% according to working temperature — the higher the temperature the less accelerator required. In average, draught-free conditions of 68°F (20°C) use 2%.
  1% add 5 ml (cc) to 1 lb resin.
  2% add 10 ml (cc) to 1 lb resin.
  3% add 15 ml (cc) to 1 lb resin.
  4% add 20 ml (cc) to 1 lb resin.

The above amounts are given using Scott Bader

accelerator E. Check manufacturer's instructions if
using another type.

Use separate mixing measures for catalyst and
accelerator. For thicker castings of $\frac{1}{8}$" upwards —
decrease accelerator. As little as 0·5% ml (cc) per lb
of resin can be enough. For castings of $\frac{1}{2}$" upwards
it may be necessary to reduce the catalyst as well.
0·5% catalyst and the same amount of accelerator
can be tried as a starting point. If it has not gelled
after several hours, it can be gradually hardened by
the gentle application of warm air (fan heater, etc.)

**Make tests and record mixtures as you make
them up.**
Note that the minimum working temperature is
59°F (15°C) for successful results.

Metric Weights.
With the increasing use of metric standards it is
advisable to buy metric weights. These also simplify
the percentage calculations when measuring
catalysts and accelerators as a proportion of the resin.
For example:
    1% of 2,800 grams of resin — 28 cc.
    2% of 2,800 grams of resin — 56 cc.
Downland (K & C Mouldings – see Material Suppliers)
supply both scales and metric weights.
Some catalysts are supplied in paste form. These have
an advantage in that they can be 're-activated' by
heat once mixed with the resin, so that if the
temperature did drop (say overnight) and the mix
chilled below a working temperature, it would be
certain to start to polymerize once warmed. But the
difficulty of measuring and using paste generally
means that the liquid is more suitable for workshop
use.

EPOXY RESIN

The epoxide or epoxy resins are derived from ethylene oxide and were first patented as adhesives in 1945. They have outstanding mechanical properties coupled with an extremely low shrinking rate, which makes a very good adhesive and casting agent for use with glass. The surface quality of epoxy is harder and more glass-like in quality than polyester. The standard epoxy resin commonly used has an amber colour and has its place where richly-coloured glasses are being used. But if clarity is required, two special 'water white' types are now available, the American Stycast 1264 and the British Araldite MY 790 (see details in Appendix). Stycast is supplied, as are most epoxies, as a two-part mix of base resin and catalyst and is slightly flexible in thin section, which is an advantage when used with glass. The white Araldite resin is also supplied as a two-part material, but if a slightly flexible quality is required, it is supplied separately in the form of a liquid plasticiser (DY 040). When used to stick or embed glass the plasticiser should be added to the Araldite. Of the two resins, the Araldite is clearer, its hardener (X83/319) being very clear, while the Stycast catalyst has a very slight green/yellow cast.

The base resin is usually found to be set in a hard white crystalline state when the container is opened. Before the catalyst is mixed in, the base resin must be heated until it becomes absolutely clear and liquid, otherwise the curing process may not take place properly. It is easily warmed in front of a fan heater, the required temperature advised by Araldite being 122°–131°F (50°–55°C). Once clear and free running, it is advisable to allow to cool to 95°F (35°C), or as near to this temperature as possible without it crystallising again. At this point the hardener should be added whilst continuously stirring the mixture. Where castings over 100 grams are being made, it is advisable to place the container

in a shallow dish or bowl of water in order to bring
the temperature of the mixture down to room
temperature. The usable life of a 250 gram (just over
$\frac{1}{2}$ lb) resin mix is about 3 hours at (68°F) 20°C.
But if larger amounts of mixed resin are allowed to
stand in one bulk, exothermic reaction is liable to take
place which will shorten the usable life of the
material. This can happen quite suddenly and leave
the user with a container of rapidly solidifying, hot,
smoking resin, turning a deep amber in colour. A
method of ensuring that this does not happen is to
pour the large bulk into several smaller containers
where the mixture can spread out into a thinner layer
(5–10 mm) which radically reduces the heat build-up.
From this it will be seen that thicker castings will take
less time to gel and harden. Where very thin layers are
used I find it an advantage not to reduce the
temperature from 50–55°C at the time of mixing but
keep the warmer temperature. Pouring out the liquid
onto a large area very quickly dissipates the heat and
if it cools too much it takes a much longer time to
harden. At room temperature 68°F (20°C) the resin
can take 48 hours to cure. This is reduced by the
application of heat, bearing in mind the points already
made on castings of more than 100 grams. Thin
surface coats will need the help of radiant or fan
heaters, if they are to harden in 24 hours. Where free
forms of glass are made up using this material as a
bonding agent, it is sometimes an advantage to
allow the resin to gel to a treacle-like consistency.
It is then easier to use as a glue and allows more
bonding to be carried out, without resin running out
from the bonded areas. Some care has to be taken to
keep the resin under observation to see that it is used
at the right time. Usually, a mix made late in the
afternoon and kept in smaller amounts will be ready
for use during the next day – but a mix made in the
morning can be too liquid later on in the day and may
be solid and unusable by the following morning.

Plate 15
(a) Cutting. Mechanical textured
glass, different types juxtaposed in
controlled area, to act as second
layer of double sided artificially lit
interior screens. All the glass is
thoroughly washed to remove
grease and dirt before use.

(b) Marking the subsidiary cut
lines and laying up textured glass
on $\frac{1}{4}$" georgian wired polished
plate panel over coloured antique
layer already bonded to the reverse
side. Only the main contour cut
lines of the design are drawn up
full size from the beginning; the
secondary cut lines within these
pre-determined areas are evolved
whilst working.

(c) Checking a series of cut pieces. Whilst glass appliqué does not follow the same rules of accurate cutting as for lead glazing, unless it is close butted, it does need far more control than is sometimes thought.

(d) Studio set-up for glass appliqué. Showing a closed light box central and each side of this open Dexion frames with thick industrial felt covering on top edges. The far frame with white plastic reflective surface below and movable spot lighting is for laying up, and the one in the foreground, which has three accessible sides, although also used for laying up as shown is mainly used for bonding. This again has reflective surface below, movable spots and a 3 kW blower heater to heat glass for bonding and control humidity.

(e) The bonding material used is Araldite epoxy resin. Resin AY103 in 1 lb tins and hardener HY951 in 2 oz bottles is clinically mixed in the required proportions using 20 ml hypodermic to measure accurately the pre-heated resin and a 2 ml hypodermic to measure the hardener. Clean polythene cups are used for each mix, enough to easily handle without fear of gelling, and cleaned for re-use with cellulose thinners and heavy duty dispensable paper towels. Nitromors water-soluble paint remover is excellent for cleaning off unwanted dry resin from surface of glass.

(f) All glass is removed from plate panel for bonding and stacked in separate layers on a movable board alongside. The plate glass receives a final clean and is heated by the 3 kW blower below. The $\frac{1}{4}''$ georgian wired polished plate has all edges covered before use with heavy duty waterproof tape. This establishes the area to be left clear for glazing bars and also allows for easy handling with no risks. Masking tape is used to form boundaries to the areas to be treated with glass appliqué and glass is handled by the edges only and checked to avoid the transfer of grease or moisture from the hands.

(g) Settling of each piece of glass is important, pressing down to eliminate all air bubbles for visual as well as the practical reasons of expansion of trapped air which can cause breakages.

(h) The start of a panel being bonded, showing taped edges, masked areas, syringe and polythene cup with epoxy mix. Glass is bonded by working steadily across panel.

(i) Bonding completed and hardened, masking removed and surplus resin cleaned from surface of glass and in between where it would inhibit grouting:

(j) Detail of completed panel with second lamination of textured glass on reverse side to antique colour which has now been grouted with a dark cement filler. It also shows the designer mark etched into one of the pieces within the clear area.
Photos and captions by courtesy of Ray Bradley.
(See plate 5 for full colour photograph of this work in situ, page 14).

Formulations of Stycast and Araldite Resins:

Stycast 1264.   Base Resin (Part A)
                 100 parts by weight.
                 Hardener (Part B)
                 45 parts by weight.

Araldite.   Base Resin (MY 790)
                 100 parts by weight.
                 Hardener (X83/319)
                 24 parts by weight.
                 Plasticiser (DY 040)
                 20 parts by weight.

Care must be taken to ensure that mixing instruments do not come into contact with any base resin once they have been used in the hardener resin mix. The uncured resin materials should not come into contact with food stuffs, food utensils, or the skin. Barrier creams, protective polythene or rubber gloves should be used, particularly by people with sensitive skin, as they could be affected. When work is finished, soap and hot water should be used to wash any areas that have come into contact with resin and the use of a resin-removal cream is advisable. (See materials section.) Acetone or cellulose thinners are suitable cleaning agents for unhardened resin on tools but they should not be used on the skin. Disposable clean tins are best used for mixing purposes.

Whilst working with the resin, a supply of paper towels is useful for wiping the hands, Do not use cloth towels.

The hardener gives off some fumes when the container lid is opened and if used in considerable bulk a well ventilated area should be used for mixing, etc.

Epoxy should have a shelf life of at least 12 months if stored in a cool, dry place. In practice, I have found that the base resin will last a long time, but the hardener is more likely to deteriorate at a faster rate, especially in temperatures in excess of (68°F) 20°C.

For this reason it is always advisable to make small test samples on materials which have been held in store for several months.

Colouring pastes are available for use with Epoxy resins (see Material Suppliers). The majority make the resin opaque, but the red, green and blue of the Araldite range are translucent dyes. The manufacturers' instructions should be carefully followed when using these pigments, but the basic points to note are that the base resin should be warmed up to (248°F) 120°C to allow uniform distribution of the paste and the amount of hardener should be increased in proportion to the amount of paste used.

Generally it will be found that coloured translucent forms will be more readily produced using polyester resins. The epoxy is best used as a surface coat over these as described in Chapter Three.

ACRYLIC

When maximum clarity is required, it is possible to buy acrylic (methyl methacrylate) in liquid form, supplied with a separate hardener. This is a partially polymerised 'syrup'; the hardener being added to complete the process of transforming the acrylic into the clear solid material, well known, when produced commercially by I.C.I. or Röhm & Haas, as Perspex or Plexiglas, respectively.

Two products sold as acrylic sheet and block bonding adhesive both work well as casting material for glass panels. Acrifix 90 (Röhm & Haas) and Tensol No. 7 (I.C.I.) are both suitable for thicker castings and embedments. But when used for the adhesion of thin glass sheets (glass appliqué) there is a tendency for de-lamination to take place some weeks after the mixture has hardened. Acrifix 93 (Röhm & Haas) remains permanently elastic and is advised by the manufacturers for the bonding of glass and acrylic sheeting, but it has a slight yellow colour.

I have not found as much heat build-up in Acrifix 90 or Tensol No. 7 as there is in polyester during the polymerisation period, after the hardener is added, although some contraction takes place in the material. It is an exciting material to use on its own in the creation of clear forms. As it is supplied in a syrup-like consistency, air bubbles tend to stay in the mixture unless the air is removed in a vacuum chamber. As Acrifix and Tensol are used for bonding both clear and coloured acrylic block and sheet, this can be used in conjunction with glass, or on its own.

Acrylic is more expensive than polyester, but competitive with epoxy.

Tests using acrylic as a surface layer on top of a polyester and glass slab, in place of the epoxy resin described in Chapter 4, have proved successful; a faster setting time being achieved. Epoxy has a harder surface, however, and is less prone to surface scratching. The surface hardness of acrylic is similar to that of aluminium.

Clear embedding techniques can be effectively carried out in acrylic. For detailed instructions the Information Sheets issued by I.C.I. and Röhm & Haas (see Material Suppliers Appendix) are very useful.

REINFORCEMENTS

Various works, especially the larger panels and free forms, will require strengthening materials of various types to be included in their structure.

In the majority of the work illustrated in this book the two kinds most commonly used are glass fibre and steel or alloy bars, either by themselves or in combination with one another.

GLASS FIBRE

Glass fibre is obtainable in the form of chopped strand mat, woven cloth and scrim, tissue or surface mat, ribbon and individual fibres. As the name suggests, it is made by spinning fine filaments of glass into fibres which are both strong and flexible. This strength, when combined with the rigidity of a cured resin, makes it a useful reinforcement, particularly in panels. It has the advantage of becoming translucent when soaked or 'wetted out' by clear resin and can therefore be used as a base for large panels.

For the purposes of the work described in this book the chopped strand mat is the type which will be most commonly used. This is made up of short glass fibres, usually 2" long, laid together in a random pattern, and held together with resin-based binder, which disintegrates when soaked by the applied resin, leaving the glass fibres held in the laminate.

There are various thicknesses, textures and qualities of the mat available, and for translucent work it is advisable that an 'E' type mat is obtained from the manufacturer. This is of the low-alkali variety and leaves no trace of fibre pattern in the completed laminate. An 'A' type mat, suitable for opaque coloured laminates, may leave a fibre pattern in clear resin. This is less expensive, but does not weather as

Plate 16
Glass fibre (in the form of chopped strand mat) being placed in wooden former, previously lined with polythene.

well in exterior work. Thickness is given by weight per square foot. Either 1 oz, $1\frac{1}{2}$ oz or 2 oz per square foot are commonly available. These are made up in rolls of 36″ or 54″ width and a full roll will usually weigh from 60 to 100 lbs. Where off-cuts are obtained from firms using glass fibre, it would be important to check that the right kind of mat is being provided if an 'E' type is required. For general use, a 1 oz mat will be useful, as two or more layers can be used where thicker laminates are wanted. Obviously, the thicker the layer of glass fibre, the greater the strength, but increasing the thickness makes for less clarity in a cast or laminate. This quality can be turned to use where artificial back illumination is used as the glass fibre acts as a light-diffusing layer. (See Chapter 4).

METAL REINFORCEMENTS

Practically any metal bar, rod or wire can be used, embedded in a form, to give rigidity and strength. The type and size of material used will depend on the size of the actual work – the author has made free works

Plate 17
Metal reinforcement framework of
welded $\frac{3}{8}''$ square steel bar, lying
in polythene-lined wooden former,
ready for glass and concrete. The
finished panel is shown in Plate 29,
p. 97.

in one piece up to 18 feet in length. This is made
possible by the use of mild steel bar, $\frac{3}{4}'' \times \frac{1}{8}''$ in
section, which was welded into a support frame work
and set onto a glass fibre base layer. (See photos of
National Provincial Commission, Plates 25 and 35.) For
free standing work a fabricated frame is advisable.
The successful design of a structure will depend very
much on whether or not the support frame-work
has been well considered. It should be considered as
the foundation of the form, and not be worked out as
an afterthought.

Where support frames are wanted in larger works
using slab glasses, especially in free work,
considerable weight can be involved and it is useful
to have welding apparatus to form an integral
framework. Either oxy-acetylene or electric arc
welders are suitable. I find that a small 110 amp
electric arc welder is very efficient in being able to be
used to quickly 'tack' weld a form to its final shape
before being used to completely weld up the joints.
(See Equipment, Chapter 5.)

Plate 18 (opposite)
White slab glass set edge-on into
1" thickness of clear epoxy with
aluminium bright tubes laid
between the glass sections and
embedded in the resin. Tubes can
extend either end and become part
of the fixing structures.
(Photo: George Perks)

A great variety of welding rods are available from stockists which enable a variety of metals to be welded both to themselves and in some cases, to each other, e.g. steel can be welded to cast iron. Aluminium is weldable using oxy-acetylene, or with a carbon arc torch working off an electric arc welder. Bright aluminium looks very well in rod or bar form set into clear laminates.

Opaque resin or concrete panels can be reinforced with welded mild steel frames for larger works. Smaller sizes can be strengthened with 12 or 14 gauge galvanised wire pieces laid around the glass pieces. When mild steel is set into concrete it should be treated with a primer to avoid rust marks showing through, especially where it is less than 1" from the surface of the panel. Steel need not be treated when set in resin, as this will permanently seal in any rust.

3
EQUIPMENT

FOR WORKING GLASS

The basic equipment needed to start work in both glass and resin is fairly simple.

Glass cutting – a glass cutter of the wheel type for scoring the surface of both antique/sheet and slabs. The line is made with a firm stroke. In the case of the thinner material it is tapped underneath the length of the line and the piece can be broken by giving a sharp breaking movement with the hands. The glass is held at one end whilst making this movement (see illustrations). Pincers are used to nip off any pieces on cuts with a concave edge.

The slabs are cut by firmly holding the glass in both hands, cut line uppermost, and giving a sharp, firm, downward blow across a sharp edged anvil, or metal edge firmly held in a vice. A cold chisel with an edge of 2" width or so makes a useful tool for this.

The edge should be kept sharp by filing when needed. A simple anvil can be made by cutting the end off a wide cold chisel and welding it to a sturdy base plate with bolt holes drilled into it, for bolting to the work bench. Slabs may need further trimming down to size and a sharp-edged hammer is useful for this. A special tungsten steel-edged hammer is made for this purpose and is desirable, as normal steel becomes blunt quite quickly.

This tool will cut off pieces of the slab with remarkable accuracy once the basic technique is mastered. The glass is held firmly in the left hand (if right handed) while the edges are cut off with firm strokes of the hammer held in the right hand. With practice, the hammer can be used to lightly chip a score line along the surface of a slab where the required break is to be made and it can then be divided on the anvil.

Where sharp edges are present on slabs, particularly when they will come above the surface of the cast construction, the sharpness should be smoothed off with a medium file, or a very coarse abrasive paper.

Plate 19
Cutting glass sheet.
(a) The glass cutter.

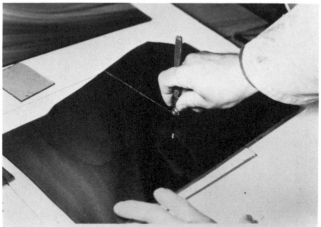

(b) Scoring the glass.

(c) Tapping from below.

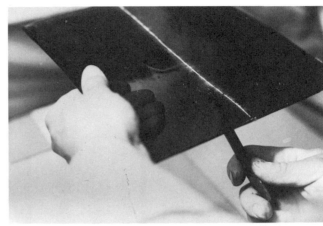

(d) Pressure from the hands.
The left hand side of the score line
is raised up on another surface,
e.g. hardboard sheet.

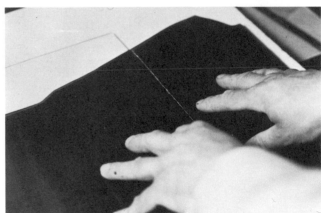

(e) Further pressure, with hands
wider apart, and the glass breaks.

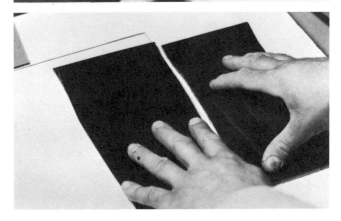

Plate 20
Cutting glass slabs.
(a) Tools in the cutting box. The three-sided box is not essential, but if used it does prevent most of the glass from spreading too far over the surface of the bench.

(b) The cutting anvil, glass cutter and tungsten-edged hammer. The anvil is made from a cold chisel cut and welded to a base plate.

(c) Pressing glass firmly onto anvil edge before making sharp downward movement.

(d) As (c), but shown from underneath glass.

(e) Making the break with a sharp downward stroke.

(f) Cutting technique using tungsten-edged hammer; in this case the slab is held on the anvil edge to give a clean, sharp cut.

(g) Edging off the slab piece with a file to remove the sharp cutting edge. Coarse carborundum paper will also carry out this job.

PROTECTIVE EQUIPMENT

Light industrial gloves and goggles should be worn when handling and chipping glass. A pair of cotton backed, leather gloves is ideal; they should give protection but not be too stiff and heavy.

Eye goggles, as illustrated, are ideal, being light and easy to use. It cannot be emphasised too strongly that these should be used at all times when glass chipping is being carried out with the hammer.

A thick canvas or leather apron is also a worthwhile requirement, particularly for beginners, as slabs can sometimes break into several pieces, fall down from the working surface and even cut clothing. Strong leather shoes are also advisable for the same reason.

Plate 21
Protective equipment.
(a) Gloves (light industrial and
polythene disposable), face visor
(at back), goggles and face mask.

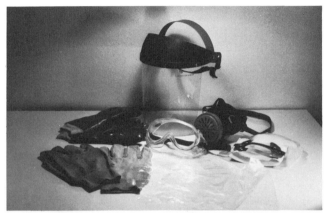

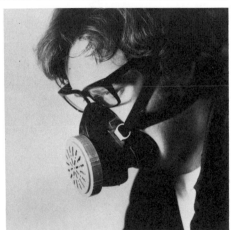

(b) (above left) Face protective
visor; protects whole face and is
especially useful for spectacle
wearers.

(c) (above right) Protective
respirator for use in fume
conditions or a dusty
atmosphere. Different filters are
available for various requirements.
Use with epoxy resins.

(d) Disposable polythene gloves.

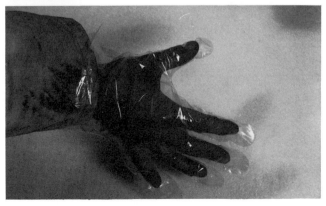

BENCH/STORAGE FOR GLASS

When slabs are being cut and chipped it will be found that the amount of glass pieces and chippings soon multiply until work becomes difficult. Boxes for storage should be obtained and it helps to be able to sort out the colours into individual containers at this stage, saving a great deal of time and trouble later. Stout cardboard boxes are suitable, but it helps to line them with thick polythene sheeting to stop small pieces dropping through the bottom.

A temporary, three-sided box, placed on the work bench, stops most of the glass spreading too far over the surface (see Plate 20a).

When large numbers of sheet and slab glasses are being used, storage racks will become necessary for easy handling and comparison between various colours. Compartments for these should allow up to 12 slabs to lie side by side. As they are 12" × 8" × 1" the depth should be 12", height not less than 10" and width will be just over 1" per slab. If space is available, allow extra width in each compartment for a box to hold smaller pieces.

Where work is of a temporary nature and carried out in a workshop or studio usually devoted to other activities, the glass can be stored in the cardboard boxes which the suppliers use for packing. They are quite strong and can be placed in rows against a wall, or on strong shelves. Each box holds 10 slabs.

EQUIPMENT FOR RESINS

Polyester resins are supplied in small quantities in cans of 1 lb upwards, or in bulk drums of 56 lb, 112 lb or approx. 500 lbs (45 gallons). Small quantities can be mixed in disposable clean tins or paper cups. Larger quantities of 2–10 lbs are easily mixed in plastic buckets, which can be obtained fairly cheaply from most ironmongers. Several of these should be bought in order that the remains of a mix can be allowed to harden off before being used again. The hardened resin can be removed by flexing the bucket, or just left on, if it is firm enough not to break up and spoil subsequent mixes in the same container. Rather than attempt to clean off liquid resin, it is far easier to catalyse it, add accelerator, if not already present, and let it harden.

All pouring operations should be carried out over cellophane or polythene sheeting, especially when the larger drums are being 'decanted'. Polythene sheeting is one of the most useful materials available when this work is being carried out and it pays to buy a full roll from a builder's merchant. It is obtainable in rolls of various sizes and thickness. Thin, medium and thick grades are available.

Smaller amounts can be bought from ironmongers.

The medium grade will be a good general choice for most work.

Cellulose sheeting

More commonly known by the trade name of 'Cellophane' of British Cellophane Ltd. Small amounts can be bought from household suppliers, but the correct grade for a polyester releasing agent is the PT grade, which is available in reels up to 92 inches wide. Three gauge thicknesses are made – PT 300, PT 400 and PT 600. PT 400 is a good standard gauge for general use.

Drum taps should be bought for the 500 lb drums, if they are ever used, as they require two or more people to move them when full. A drum trolley on wheels is also useful.

As resin will be measured by weight, a pair of scales
will be needed. The most suitable type will be the
all metal balance variety with individual weights.
These can be cleaned of surplus resin, which is more
difficult to remove from plastic household scales and
may seize them up altogether if it seeps into the
spring mechanism. As hardener/catalyst and
accelerator amounts are given as percentages of the
actual resin by weight, it is helpful to use a set of
metric weights, which can be used on the simple flat
balance type of scale.

Dispensing catalyst/hardener and accelerators should
be carried out using glass measuring cylinders, or
even better, automatic plastic dispensers. They are
both marked in cc and should be used for accurate
dispensing. As has already been stated, catalyst/
hardener and accelerator must never be mixed
directly together and they will both require separate
dispensers. Care should be taken to store these
away from heat or direct sunlight and to avoid direct
contact with each other.

Large spatulas are useful for mixing the resin with
catalyst, accelerator or pigments. Care must be taken
to have enough mixing implements to avoid having to
put one which has been in a catalyst mix back into
uncatalysed base resin. Metal rods, old hacksaw
blades or pieces of wood can make good mixing
tools, but they must be clean.

Cutting glass fibre can be carried out with sharp
cutting knives or scissors – both will be of use.
Impregnating the mat is best carried out using
brushes. Special types with solvent-resistant setting
are available in widths from $\frac{1}{2}$" to 4". $2\frac{1}{2}$" is a practical
size for most applications. It is advisable to purchase
these brushes by the dozen and it should be borne in
mind that cleaning must take place before the resin

has gelled, otherwise the brush will be unusable again. Brushes with white bristles are available and are preferable to the black bristle type, as any stray bristles show up with clear resins if they are dark in colour. Acetone, or any other specially made up solvent, obtainable from a manufacturer, is used for cleaning the ungelled resin from brushes. In addition, a proprietary household cleanser with bleach as an ingredient, or a washing detergent used in hot water will be found to be a successful (and perhaps cheaper) method of removing the worst of the resin from the brush. Care must be taken over cleaning and it is wise to keep several containers with acetone and domestic cleaners handy. Acetone only should be used for cleaning during the working period, as water must not get into any other resin being used. It is safe to use a brush which has just had gelling resin removed by cleaning in the solvent as long as no acetone can be shaken or rubbed out of the bristles.

The final cleaning of the day should be thorough, including washing with soap and warm water, and brushes should be finally stored in a clean tin with clean acetone covering the bristles. As evaporation takes place quite quickly, brushes should be checked frequently if not in use. A brush left for a day in a tin containing solvent used previously will be found to be set in the resin sediment at the bottom and may be useless for further work. Although it may not be absolutely necessary, a roller to compact the resin-soaked glass fibre, can be a useful tool. Several varieties are available – rollers with circular metal or plastic rollers or with metal 'fins' or 'paddles' are common. I prefer the fin/paddle type (see Plate 11), which breaks up any air bubble concentration by breaking the mat around it. The circular roller seems to push the air around, rather than break it out of the lamination. A mohair roller for depositing resin and consolidating a laminate, is well worthwhile for larger areas.

PROTECTIVE EQUIPMENT
AND MATERIALS FOR RESINS

Small scale work can be carried out with a minimum
of mess and cleaning, but large work will require old
clothing, including shoes. Plastic gloves protect the
hand, but can be troublesome, especially when they
become hard with gelled resin and mat. Disposable
polythene gloves are the most suitable in the
workshop.

It will be found that the majority of work is carried
out with the bare hands, protected with a barrier
cream. Kerodex 71 is a good protection against resins
and glass fibre, which can cause irritation if handled
without gloves or barrier cream.
Resin should be cleaned from the hands before it
sets hard, and a removal cream, Kerocleanse 22, is
very good for this. A little rubbed onto resin will
remove it efficiently if it has not set hard. 'Keroderm'
handcream is a useful after-treatment for those with
specially sensitive skins. Overalls or an apron help
protect clothing. It is possible to make up a good
apron from heavy duty polythene sheet.

Personally, I find that protective clothing can be too
cumbersome, and rely on old jeans and a thick twill
shirt. After several years of work with resin, the jeans
become like armour. It is interesting to see how
tenaciously drops of polyester will adhere to cloth
and survive constant washing in boiling water and
detergent!

4
GLASS
WITH RESIN

There are many advantages in the recent techniques being developed using resins to bond together antique, plate and slab glasses. From the design aspect, large forms can be produced in one piece, and there is a great deal of flexibility in colour, texture, clarity and light diffusing quality required. A major consideration from the production point of view will be the limited amount of equipment required to set up a working area. No large or expensive equipment is required to produce the work, and most of the tools required are those normally found in the smaller workshop. The main items needed are the actual materials themselves — wood and blockboard, fixing screws/bolts for mould formers, sheet cellophane and polythene for lining formers to obtain a method of releasing the cast panels or forms from moulds, a supply of glass and the resins.

The most useful piece of equipment required will be found to be a portable fan heater, especially in a draughty working area, or in cold or damp weather, which can drastically affect setting properties of the resins by retarding the rate of setting and often result in permanent 'undercure' or surface tack. (See Chapter 2.) In my workshop I have two infra-red strip heaters, which are very good, both for providing general heating and for helping the setting process when casting with resins. (See illustrations, pages 62, 63.) These, in conjunction with a fan heater, provide a good heating system.

It is most important to stress the fact that whatever formulae are given, for catalyst and accelerator proportions in an 'average' room temperature, the setting rate can be remarkably changed by draughts, humidity and temperature variations and only by personal observations in the actual working conditions will good results be obtained.

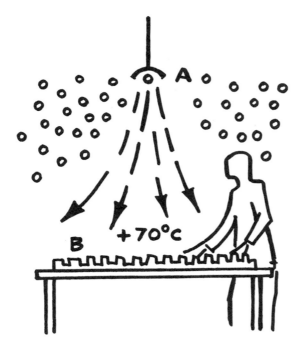

Figure 3
Two 8' long electric infra red strip heaters are suspended from ceiling, giving good local temperature at work bench level during cool weather and in damp conditions.

   *Cool air*

Warm air

A Infra red strip heater.
B Working surface.

Polyester resin, in particular, can be affected by these variations and covering with polythene sheeting is one of the best ways of overcoming the problem. A thermometer placed inside the covering sheet will indicate the exact temperature which the casting is subjected to. The reverse problem can arise in very warm weather, when excessive heat can cause overheating in the casting and the amount of accelerator has to be reduced, as mentioned in Chapter 2.

Glass panels and constructions can be formed using polyester or epoxy resins alone but I have found that an effective technique is to form the base layers of the structure with polyester — when this is cured a top layer of epoxy is laid on to complete the casting.

For quick results in making sketch models which do not have to last, a straight clear polyester resin can be used, but it will be found that cracking will eventually

Figure 4
Two methods of using fan heater.
A Fan heater.
B Working surface.
C Polythene sheet cover.

take place. This is because the coefficient of expansion of polyester resin is different from that of glass, so in order to make allowance for this the basic clear resin must be modified by the addition of a flexible resin; from 20% to 50% of flexible resin may be used. The amount will vary with the size and volume of the glass pieces – the larger the pieces, the greater the amount of flexibility required. A panel composed of small glass chips may only need 25% of flexible resin, while one with 1″ thick × 4″ long slab pieces will require 40% to 50% of flexible resin.

Although the casting is flexible enough to make up the expansion of the glass, the surface hardness will not be noticeably affected. Where flexible resin is used, an increase may be found in 'surface tack', also known as 'air inhibition'. To overcome this a special accelerator can be used (Scott Bader accelerator W).

Figure 5
(a) 25% flexible resin mix for
small glass pieces.

(b) Up to 40% flexible resin mix
for larger slabs.

It has a wax additive, which gives the final casting a
non-sticky surface. Alec Tiranti of London also sell a
wax additive for use with polyester resin.

Another solution to this problem is to coat any tacky
surface with a thin, well catalysed and accelerated
mix of clear resin, which will dry tack-free. The
manufacturers of polyester resins give tables for the
correct amount of catalyst and accelerator to be used,
under normal conditions, in the production of
glass fibre laminates. Where thicker sections are cast,
the information in Chapter 2, page 33 should be
carefully studied – where the reductions in the
amount of catalyst and/or accelerator are pointed
out, if over-heating (thermal exotherm) is not to take
place. This can result in severe stress and cracking in
the casting.

The thickness, type of resins used and the inclusion of
glass fibre mat will all affect the quality of the finished
panel or construction. The deeper the resin, the
greener the colour cast will be in the resin areas. It is
possible to tint or fully colour the polyester resins
with translucent dispersed pigments. Where a very
clear effect is wanted, a slight amount of translucent
blue pigment added to the clear resin helps to kill the

greenish colour cast and add to the clarity of the casting. But the greenish cast is not unpleasant and experiments can be made on small, full thickness, samples of resin before starting larger pieces, to see what resin colour qualities result from various tints being added to the base material.

As the surface of cast polyester does not have quite the same appearance and 'feel' as glass, the application of a top layer of an epoxy resin, as previously mentioned, is worth while. Acrylic can also be used.

Figure 6
A Waterwhite epoxy resin.
B Polyester resin.

Araldite MY 790 and Stycast 1264 (Chapter 2 – Resins) are very good for this purpose, being clear and giving a hard, glass-like surface when cured. It is advisable to let the polyester under layer cure off thoroughly before applying the epoxy, which should be treated as the method described on page 35. This resin is also excellent for making complete castings. It has approximately the same coefficient of expansion as glass and can be poured in one operation. However, it is approximately four times the cost of polyester resin, so that it becomes expensive if used in that way.

In the formation of slab glass structures epoxy is a useful bonding material, when made slightly flexible, which helps in making non-brittle joints. Glass fibre mat can be used as a background layer at the base of a cast laminate. This gives added strength to the panel and diffuses the light more than a resin layer would with no glass fibre included. This quality is particularly useful if the structure is to be used in front of an artificial system of lighting. An inch thick layer of

glass in resin, on a base layer of glass fibre mat, will
diffuse out the harsh outline of fluorescent strip
lights. The distance of the panel from the lights will
be critical and it is usually found that a gap of at
least 4″ will be needed. The greater the distance the
better the overall diffusion of light.

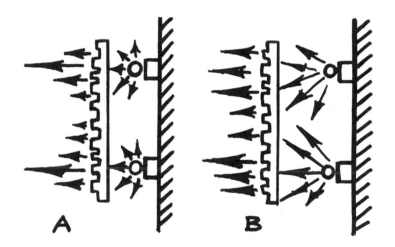

Figure 7
*A Fluorescent strip lights close to
panel.*
*B Light at least 4″ away, giving
more even light distribution.*

Where panels are used against natural daylight the
glass fibre layer can lose some of the clarity and
sparkle of the glass and it will be useful to make
small samples both with and without glass fibre, to
compare them. If glass fibre mat is used, it should be
an 'E' type, which is specially designed for use in
translucent work, as it 'wets out' well and no
individual fibres are noticeable in the completed
casting. Normal mats, used in opaque laminates, can
show fibre texture if used with transparent resin.

Plate 22(a) and (b)
Two views of the back support from an electric fitting (circular fluorescent tube) to be placed behind the panel shown in Plate 13. The side baffle panels are made in translucent polyester and glass fibre.

CONSTRUCTION OF FLAT PANELS

Simple flat panels can be made simply by making up a
base former with sides as deep, or deeper, than the
intended thickness of the resin. Small panels can be
cast in formers made with plywood or chipboard
bases but blockboard is stronger and will last longer.
Wall side strips can be nailed, screwed or bolted to
the base of the former to make up the shallow tray,
into which resins will be poured.

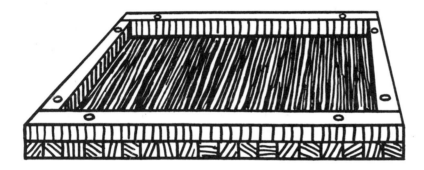

1" × 1" wood batten is adequate for making the walls
of a simple former. If absolutely straight, sharp edges
are required, all the wood and blockboard surfaces
which will be in direct contact with the resin must be
well sealed, first with at least two coats of a
cellulose (wood) filler, and then wax polished (use a
non-silicone variety, as silicones can affect the
setting properties of the polyester resin). The wax is
polished to achieve as shiny a surface as possible, in
order to gain easy release of the final casting. If this
method is used, it is necessary to allow at least two
of the wall sides of the former to be removed so that
a flat spatula or blade can be inserted between the
cast panel and the base in order to gently allow air to
release it.

Figure 8
Simple former of wood.
Sides the thickness of resin to be
cast – screwed onto blockboard
base panel.

Plate 23
Steps in the making of a simple panel.
(a) The former/mould tray is made up with 1″ × 1″ walls on ½″ block-board. This allows resin to be ¾″ in depth, with glass pieces standing above the surface to any required distance.

(b) The former is lined with sheet polythene which is allowed to overhang the sides and is held in place by clear adhesive tape.

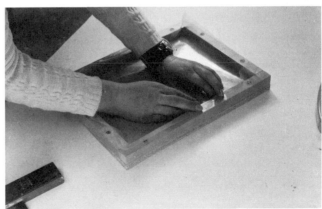

(c) Catalysed and accelerated resin layer is poured onto polythene and two layers of glass fibre mat are well impregnated with a glass fibre lay-up brush. This base layer can be allowed to harden. No flexible resin is needed in this base.

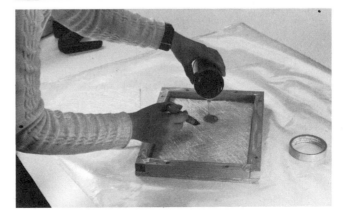

(d) 1" thick coloured glass slabs are cut, trimmed to remove sharp edges and placed in position on the base glass fibre layer. A thin layer of polyester resin, modified with flexible resin, can be poured on to hold large pieces in position.

(e) Smaller offcuts and chippings of glass are used to fill in areas between larger pieces.

(f) Polyester resin is poured – from 25% to 40% of flexible resin is added to modify this. The pouring will be best applied in two or three separate layers, alternating with glass chips.

(g) Removing the cast panel from mould when hard, usually 24 hours later.

(h) Cleaning up and filing off sharp edges to complete panel.

(i) The finished piece.

A coat of Poly Vinyl Alcohol, p.v.a., painted or sponged in a thin, even layer, over the waxed resin contact areas on the former will also help in releasing the cast form. When dry this creates a thin rubber-like film which parts the cast form from the wood with ease. Releasing from a waxed mould becomes progressively easier so that the first casting from the former could be treated with p.v.a. while later ones would release from the waxed surface alone. The p.v.a. film can be washed from the cast when it has been removed from the mould.

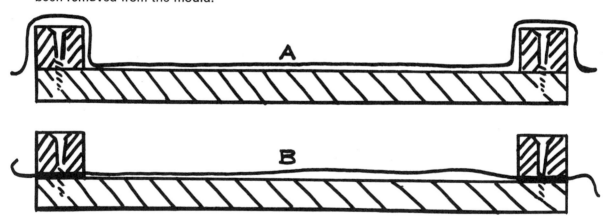

As the process of waxing, etc. and releasing from the former takes time, the use of sheet polythene or Cellophane, placed in the box mould, saves a considerable amount of time, since it also enables the cast form to be removed from the former without the removal of the sides. If dead straight sides are still needed the polythene can be stretched over the base board only, before the walls are fixed onto it. The side walls are then the only areas in need of waxing for release purposes. When the casting is complete they can be unscrewed and lightly tapped away from the cast panel, which, in turn, is just lifted from the Cellophane/polythene release sheet on the base. When panel edges do not have to be absolutely flat the interior of the former can be lined wholly with the release sheet. This method gives some very interesting

Figure 9
A Completely lining former with polythene or Cellophane.
B Base protected with polythene sheet to keep sharp sides.

effects in surface pattern and texture, to those faces with which it comes into contact.

It will be found that the thickness, type of sheeting, stretching tension of the sheeting, will all affect the type of quality that can be obtained.

Apart from providing base layers for glass panels these textured glass fibre resin sheets are an interesting source of ideas in themselves and can be used in panels and constructions in their own right. Where a laminate is made 'sandwiched' between two sheets of Cellophane or polythene very interesting forms and surface textures can result and, with practice, a good measure of control is possible. The release sheeting should be pressed into the former in one sheet, which is obviously cut to allow for the sides, in addition to an extra amount, which can be used to pull the panel from the mould.

Corners will need to be pressed in and held in position on the top edge of the mould walling by clear adhesive tape.

Two layers of sheet are advisable as a small hole in a layer can lead to resin leaking out onto the wood, which can lead to difficulties. It is as well to thoroughly inspect every inch of sheeting used to make sure that it will not leak and also to check that no small pieces of grit or glass are in the former before the sheet is inserted, as a very small particle can puncture a hole quite easily. It is advisable to give the former a quick seal with cellulose filler or wax just in case a leak does take place. This will stop the resin soaking into the wood or board. When a glass fibre base layer is wanted, it should be well 'wetted out' with resin, see Plate 23c, page 69, and it can be allowed to set first, or previously prepared glass pieces can be pressed into the wet layers. Usually, two layers of 1 oz, $1\frac{1}{2}$ oz or 2 oz chopped strand mat (CSM) make a good base layer.

Panels can be of any depth, from $\frac{1}{4}''$ thickness upwards. Thinner panels can be made up using antique, plate and/or chips of slab glasses. Slab glasses themselves are approximately 1" thick when used flat. It will be seen that the maximum amount of light refraction will be gained when the glass breaks through the resin surface, so a panel of slabs will

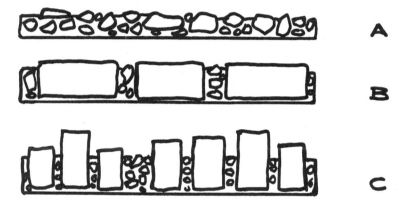

A

B

C

probably be most effective with the glass standing proud of the resin areas. Slabs may also be used on edge to stand in deep relief from the resin area. When slabs are cut and trimmed down to size the resulting smaller pieces and chips of glass should be carefully stored for use in filling the areas around the larger slab pieces.

It is essential that the glass used in conjunction with resin is very clean and free from grease and the easiest way to ensure this is to wash the slabs before they are cut and trimmed into smaller pieces. Washing with a grease-removing detergent of the household variety in warm water and brushing the glass in this solution will usually be adequate. When the glass is rinsed and dry, it should be handled as little as possible with bare hands, to avoid the grease which will be transferred to the glass. The disposable

Figure 10
A Thin panel using chips, plate or antique glass.
B Slab sections used flat.
C Slab sections used on edge.

Plate 24
Washing the glass to remove grease.

polythene gloves are useful for this purpose. Once a slab has been cleaned, the pieces which are cut from it can be safely used if they are stored wrapped in polythene sheet to keep them free of dust, etc. All the chipping work carried out on slabs should be carried out only when protective goggles are being worn. (See Chapter 3.) It is useful to have several boxes or tins with various colours and sizes of glass chippings for infilling the resin areas between larger pieces. Where smaller pieces are breaking through the surface there will probably be some chipping and filing to be carried out in order to remove very sharp points of glass, or knife-like edges. Bearing this in mind, it helps to have the graded pieces, so that fairly harmless pieces are used for this surface layer. When the large slab pieces are cut and trimmed to size it saves time later to file off any very sharp edges which are found at that stage. If a top coating layer of water-white epoxy is to be used, it is advisable to chip down or file off any sharp glass edges when the polyester underlayer is hard, so that there is no cleaning to carry out once the surface has been coated finally. It also helps to pay special attention to the sides and top edges of any slabs or lumps of

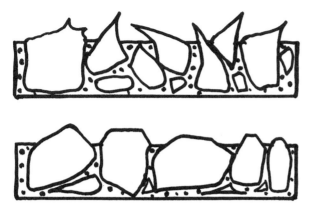

Figure 11

Bad surface edges.

Good surface edges.

glass above the resin level to see that no resin has spilled on to them. This can remain as a tacky thin layer, or if hard, start to peel away from the surface layer and it is advisable to clean it off before the final, glass-like, epoxy resin is applied.

There are an infinite number of permutations that can be used in these techniques and dark opaque areas of filled resin can be applied if required, together with other materials like sand, which can be mixed into a mortar with polyester resin and applied in bulk, or on the surface of a panel, to give a textured opaque area.

Plate 25
Sequence of panel designed and executed by the author for the National Provincial (now National Westminster) Bank, Architects, Mr F. Norman James, ARIBA, A.A.Dip. and Mr R. Sandford. By courtesy of the Bank authorities.

(a) Steel back supporting frame with supporting rods lying on wooden former. The top ends of the rods are drilled and tapped to take holding bolts, which are holding down tubular 'collars'. These collars will be embedded in the resin.

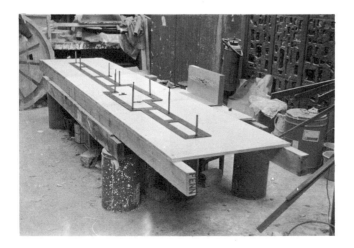

(b) The support frame is fixed under the wooden former, which has holes drilled to allow the bolts through. Collars remain on the top surface of the board, to be linked with steel bars up to $\frac{1}{8}''$ thick – these are welded to themselves and to the collars. By this method, the fixing holes in the completed form register accurately with the supporting rods.

(c) When completely welded together and cleaned up, the internal construction support frame is lifted up and a clear resin and glass fibre laminate is laid up on polythene on top of the board. Before this has set, the frame is placed on top and pressed down into this layer. Care is taken to ensure that the collars register with the drilled holes in the former. The holding bolts are then screwed through down into the supporting frame rods underneath. The support frame remains bolted to the top form as it is built up. Glass is then added.

(d) Detail of slab and antique glasses placed in position between framework and on top of laminate. Infill pieces are then added.

(e) The resin is poured in after the edges of the polythene sheeting have been raised over blocks to prevent it from pouring away.

(f) The cast resin is trimmed back to the glass form. Sharp-edged hammers and chisels are used. Note that protective goggles are being worn.

(g) Detail – edging.

(h) When the shape is resolved, the sharp edges are filed and trimmed ready for the final surface coat of clear epoxy resin.

(i) After the construction has been completed, the bolts have to be unscrewed (usually they are covered in cast resin which has to be cut away from over them). The support frame drops away and the construction is lifted up. The support frame is placed on top of the wood former, when the construction is placed directly on top of it and bolted down, if required, at this stage.

(j)   Lighting units (in this case fluorescent strips which are cool) are placed under the glass and resin form and experiments are made to determine the most satisfactory positions. The light units can be fixed either to the frame or onto the wall, when the support frame is fixed.

For transportation, the support frame is again positioned on the underside of the former, with the glass form being bolted to it through the wood. This gives a firm fixing. Note that the 'walls' of the wooden former have to be at least as deep as the overall depth of the metal supporting frame. Any wall should be carefully checked by a qualified person to ensure that it will take the weight fixed to it.

(See page 105 for full colour photograph of the finished object.)

5
GLASS
AND METAL
CONSTRUCTIONS

Glass in slab and sheet form can be set into a supporting framework of any rigid material. The most common example is, of course, the ordinary glazed window where sheet glass is fixed into a wood or metal frame and sealed with putty. As metal is available in bar, rod and sheet form which can be fabricated into strong but visually delicate constructions, it makes an excellent combination when used with sheet or slab glass. Forms can be created where the main interest is in the mass of glass, which is supported by an underlying metal support frame, or where the metal and glass are used together to create a free structure – screen construction or three-dimensional form. In the latter case, the areas of glass can be exploited to contrast or combine in space, producing free and exciting visual effects.

The main technical consideration in this technique is how the metal, be it steel, iron or aluminium, is to be fixed together. Small, light works can be made using wires or light bars that are able to be soldered or brazed. Work of any weight or size will require the basic structure to be welded together. Oxy-acetylene or electric arc welders are usually required for larger pieces. It is not too difficult to become familiar enough with welding techniques to produce work. Welding courses at local Technical Colleges or Schools are the best way of gaining the basic knowledge required and local firms using or selling welding equipment can also be very helpful in giving advice. Where a school or college wants to start work in metal/glass, there is usually a welder in the metalwork section of the craft workshop.

Mild steel bar is easy to weld and is fairly cheap, beside being available in varying widths and thicknesses.

With oxyacetylene, a flame torch, burning a mixture
of oxygen and acetylene from cylinders, heats the
pieces of metal to be joined until they are able to
receive molten metal from a welding rod, also heated
in the flame and dipped into a flux powder. The
electric arc method is made up of a transformer box
with two leads attached; one has a hand grip to
take electric welding rods, covered with a layer of
flux composition – the other is the earth lead and has
a spring clamp at the end. The earth is clamped to
one of the pieces of the metal to be welded. When
the current is switched on the welding rod attached
to the other lead is touched against the earthed
metal and an electric circuit is produced. The spark
which jumps between the end of the rod and the
metal melts the rod and the metal, thereby creating a
molten area between the two pieces to be welded,
which is filled with the metal from the rod.

The working temperature can be in the region of
1300°C. A hand mask with special dark glass and
protective gloves are essential for use with an arc
welder as the eyes will be damaged by exposure to
the direct flash caused by the striking of an electric
arc. A mask will protect both head and neck, as well
as eyes, and it is as well to wear long sleeves in order
to avoid the rays which are given off by the flash. An
advantage of the electric arc method is the speed
with which work can be lightly 'tacked' together
before being completely welded up. With practice and
a steady hand, clean, even joints can be achieved by
running the rod (electrode) along with a slight 'side
to side' motion to allow the metal to run evenly.

With an arc welder, it is possible to attach a carbon
arc torch to the terminals on the transformer. This is a
versatile tool, using carbon rods, which produces an
electric flame, permitting the brazing, annealing and
welding of metals.

Plate 26
Sequence of work in a glass and
metal construction.
(a) $\frac{3}{8}''$ bars (square steel) laid out
to suggest the form.

(b) Bars lightly tack welded.

(c) Welding up the completed
form with an electric arc welder.
Note the earth clamp on the left
and the hand grip holding the
electrode poised ready to 'strike'
an arc.

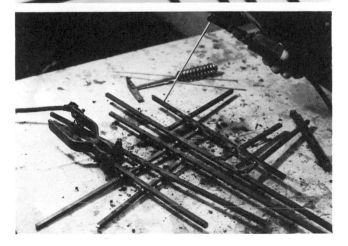

(d) Base of two 2″ × ¼″ metal bars welded on and cleaned up with grinder.

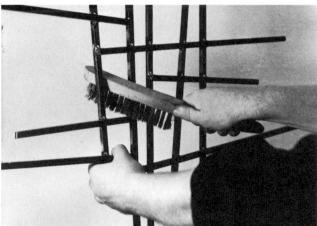

(e) Cleaning up metalwork with stiff wire brush. Ash can be removed from welds with pointed hammer.

(f) Glass cut to the required size for the shape to be filled.

(g) Mixing polyester mortar. Colour darkens as the paste hardener is mixed in.

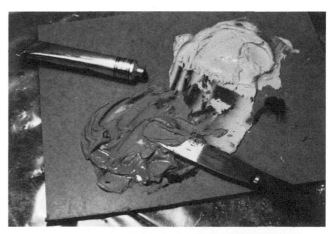

(h) Grouting in the glass with mortar.

(i) Cleaning up hardened mortar edges with a file.

*(j)   Painting metal and resin areas
with matt black paint.
(See page 108 for a full colour
photograph of the completed
construction.)*

Specialised books on welding should be consulted
for detailed methods and especially for the effects of
the pull or warping which can take place on welding
metal. This must be allowed for and can be overcome
by rigid clamping or off-setting the angle to be
welded to allow for the contraction which takes
place.

The weld produced by the arc method is left with a
black ash deposit on the surface. This is removed by
chipping away with a pointed hammer. If it is not
removed rust can develop underneath and spread out
from the joint. A stiff wire brush is also necessary
for efficient cleaning of welds.

Interesting textures can be achieved by building up
welds on the surface of the metal. A piece of sculpture
shown in the photograph (Plate 27) was made by
welding together four or five flat pieces of $\frac{1}{8}''$ thick
mild steel at a time and then welding over the inner
surfaces. The heat which was built up as the metal
from the electrode was deposited on the surface of the
bars resulted in the contraction of the inner surface –

Plate 27
Shell form, metal sculpture by the
author. (Photo: Nicholas Horne)

pulling the shape into a gentle curve. When several sections had been produced in this way they were welded together to complete the shell-like form. In this case both form and texture were produced by the same method and no mechanical bending was used at all.

If no welding facilities are available it is possible to use bars of steel etc. combined in glass and resin forms – leaving lengths protruding from the cast form for use as legs which can be fitted into a base of wood or concrete. Drilling and bolting flat bars together is another method of making up a structure to take glass, and there is no reason why work cannot be made from wood if metal is not available.

BONDING GLASS TO METAL

Glass can be fixed into the framework with a resin mortar. Several proprietary brands are readily available, being sold for body repair work on cars. They have the consistency of a thick cream and are two-pack mixes i.e. they comprise the actual base mortar, which is usually a filled polyester resin, light grey in colour, and the hardener. Hardeners come either in liquid or paste form and are simply added and mixed into the required amount of base material. Setting times can be made faster by the addition of more hardener. The average settings vary between 10 and 20 minutes. It is easy to judge the amount of hardener by eye as it changes the colour of the mortar. Any parts not mixed in enough show up by the lack of colour change. The manufacturers issue directions as to the amounts of hardener for varying setting times, but these will again depend on the working temperature. In very cold weather increase the amounts of hardener and make tests with small mixes to make sure that the timing is satisfactory.

Glass pieces should be cut slightly smaller than the spaces into which they are to be bonded. It is better to lightly bond in the glass with a small amount of fast setting mortar so that the hands are left free for the mixing and application to the space between the glass and the metal. This can be a messy job and cleaning up and removal of unwanted mortar from the glass surface is best carried out when it has set but has not completely hardened. At this stage it is like a hard rubber and can be cut and trimmed with sharp knives and rubbed off from the glass with a damp cloth. Cleaning as you work will save hours of hard labour later when the resin mortar has hardened.

It is possible to mix your own mortar, using commercial fillers which can be added to ordinary polyester resin, but generally the ready mixed filler paste mortars (e.g. Isopon, Tetrosyl, Cataloy) will be found to be more convenient and possibly stronger.

The one difficulty from the design point of view is the fact that the creation of a glass in metal form is broken down into the two stages, where the metal construction has to be made first and the glass added after. It is sometimes difficult to know when the metal construction stage is completed as the form will not be visually correct until the glass has been bonded in.

Generally, the metal construction should look light and incomplete as the addition of the tinted areas of glass with the increased visual weight given by the bonding material will radically alter the whole appearance of the form. Bonding joints can be left in the natural grey colour, or more usually are stained down with a mixture of blackboard paint with turps or white spirit. This also makes a good finish for mild steel, which should be cleaned down well and given at least one coat of a good metal primer before painting matt black.

Steel can be supplied either with a bright finish or with the greyish black mill scale still on its surface. The bright steel is more expensive. When the black is used care must be taken to see that it is well cleaned down and a good metal primer and finish coat is used, as rust can develop and spread under the mill scale on the actual surface of the metal. If a work is to be sited in the open air, the steel should be cleaned down to the bare metal and a primer be applied immediately before oxidisation takes place on the surface. Shot blasting and application of hot zinc spray or hot galvanising process are useful if carried out well. However well it is painted, mild steel will eventually rust through in the open air if not treated with either of these methods.

Plate 28(a)
Sculpture in steel and glass 3' high
with metal base, by the author.
(Photo: Nicholas Horne)

Free standing work will have to be considered
carefully to make provision for an adequate base.
Wherever possible, the base or standing bars should
be formed as an integral part of the overall design
and not be left as an afterthought.

Plate 28(b)
Flying form, sculpture by the
author, shows stone base.
(Photo: Nicholas Horne)

A piece constructed on a single stem will need a base that can safely support the mass of glass, metal and resin. It can be welded up in metal, as in the example shown (Plate 28) or the stem can be let into a block of wood, stone or concrete. In this case the block will need to be deep and heavy enough to support the weight above. Generally, a metal base will be lighter in appearance.

The screen construction in Plate 37 is an example of a free, metal form with glass where the legs are an integral part of the design. It was made from a basic idea roughly sketched on a small scale – the pieces

being welded up intuitively as and when it was
felt that they were needed. While it is possible to
design a piece completely before actually starting the
physical work, it is much more exciting and testing
to create it directly from the materials at hand. This
can lead to the creation of work with life and
freedom, worked out in terms of the materials
themselves. The 'accidental' quality of the shape or
size of a bar of steel or piece of glass will give rise

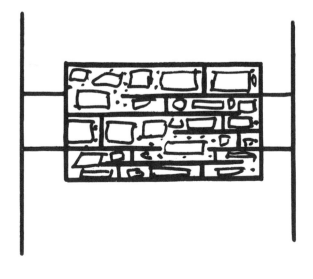

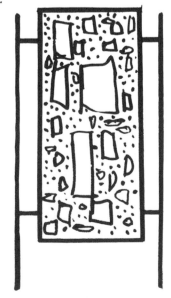

Figure 12
Three methods of mounting
suspended panels in framework.
Large work can have a metal
frame cast into the panel edge
which can be drilled and tapped to
take supporting rods or bars.
Joints should be brazed or welded
if considerable weight is involved.
See plates 31 and 32 for details
of a panel in which the metal
framework becomes part of the
design.

to a feeling that it can be used in a certain way. It may trigger off an idea which will be the basis of a construction; in other words, the materials are working on the sensibilities of the creator, who, if he is at all receptive or sensitive, will respond and use

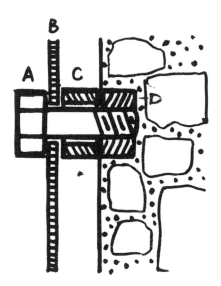

Figure 13
Three methods of fixing glass and resin panels with space between the edge and the frame.
A Bolt ($\frac{1}{4}$" upwards for 1" thickness of resin).
B Holding framework, bar or sheet (see photos of lighting unit).
C Spacing washer to hold panel from framework.
D Nut embedded in edge of panel (centre thread).

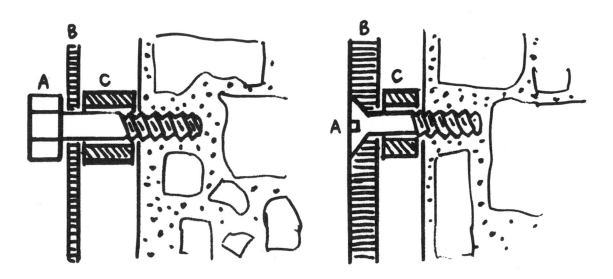

them in their own right, not straining their design
limitations by attempting to make literal
representations of natural forms.

Screens in steel and glass are very effective and can
be fixed without much trouble. Large areas can be
spanned with relatively small quantities of material,
in contrast to the glass and resin technique, as the
spaces between the metal and glass areas will work
as part of the overall design. Areas of glass and resin
can also be incorporated into metal frame works,
either by bonding in with polyester mortar or by
drilling through metal members and letting bolts
through into nuts cast into the resin of the laminate.
The cast lighting unit slab of glass (Plates 22 and 24)
is fixed in this manner – the bolts being covered with
a wax releasing agent and the ends being placed
into a hole made in the laminate which is filled with
a small amount of resin. The thread is therefore cast
into the resin – the bolt can be unscrewed and
replaced when the slab is in position. Casting in
the actual metal nut is probably better when larger,
heavier units are used. (See Figure 13.)

GLASS WITH CONCRETE OR FILLED RESINS

This is the most well known and widely used
technique of incorporating slab glasses into window
and walling panels. It was developed in France,
where it was used before World War II, and has been
widely used in Britain and the U.S.A. in both
religious and secular buildings. Although a
development from the traditional stained glass
technique it is a medium in its own right and
generally requires a much broader, less detailed
treatment than can be obtained with the painted and
leaded antique glass. As the individual 1″ thick slab

pieces are set into a solid surrounding concrete there will obviously be more marked dark intermediate areas. Just as space can be used to set off the glass in metal areas, mentioned in the previous section, so darker panel areas can be used to set off areas of glass in this technique. It is particularly relevant when used in modern buildings, as the size, texture and colour of the panel material can be designed as an integral part of the whole structure.

Glass in concrete. There are variations on the basic method, which is basically the setting of pieces of slab glass into a tray and pouring a mix of concrete around them. When cured, the tray is removed leaving a decorative panel. This is most readily carried out when the concrete is made to the exact thickness of the glass, so that a completely flush panel is formed. It will be seen that simple, small panels can be made easily in this way, but the casting formers or frames of most work will require to be made so that they can easily be taken to pieces to ensure easy releasing of the casting. Several types of casting frame can be made up, depending on the quality of surface that is wanted on the underside (generally this will be the outside surface).

Figure 14
(Above) Flush panel 1" thick.
(Below) Panel with one surface with rebated glass surfaces. Concrete mix held back by putty/plasticine walls until set.
A Wood frame.
B Plate glass rebated into wood support frame.
C Slab glass.
D Concrete – resin – sand mix.
E Plasticine or putty support walls to hold back concrete when panel thickness is deeper than glass.

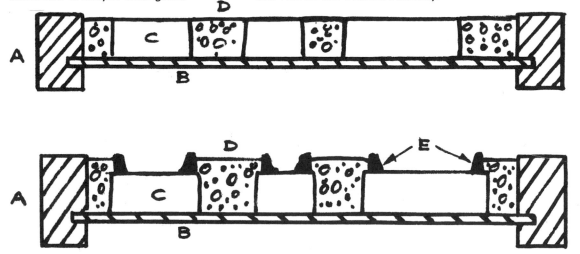

For a panel with one very smooth, polished surface
a wooden supporting frame should be made up,
rebated to allow a plate glass floor to be held in the
edges. The pieces of slab glass are placed on the glass
floor of the frame. It is advisable to lightly stick these
down with Durofix, or a similar adhesive, which will
keep the pieces in position while the concrete mix
is being tamped down, but will pull away easily when
the cast panel is released from the glass backing
sheet.

Formers of the type already shown in the previous
section on glass and resin can be made, with
polythene sheeting stretched over the base. Releasing
the cast panel is made easier, but an amount of
surface creasing usually occurs with polythene which
can mark the under surface. This can be used as a
definite surface finish — the amount of creasing
growing in proportion to the slackness of the sheeting.
If a very smooth surface is wanted on the back cast
surface of the panel the first mix of the concrete
should be a fairly wet mix, rich in cement.
Strengthening bars of thick galvanised wire should
be laid in the centre of the panel, especially where
there are thin intermediate areas of concrete between
the coloured glass pieces. Steel or strong alloy bars
should be used to strengthen larger panels. It is
advisable to coat steel bars with a primer coat to
avoid possible rust marks showing through, if they
are less than 1" from the surface of the panel.

While it may be felt that, aesthetically, panels and
glass should be cast flush on both sides (see
illustration A) there are applications where the glass
pieces may be required to be set in from the surface.
This is carried out by building a barrier of putty or
Plasticine around the edge of each piece of glass on
its top surface and casting a thicker concrete section
around it. Another method is to place cut slab glasses

Plate 29 (opposite)
*Panel, 8' × 4'. Metal reinforcement
is embedded in a panel of glass
and white Ciment Fondu. See
Plate 17, page 46. The surface
texture was achieved by tooling
the panel before the Ciment Fondu
had set.
(Gleneagles Hotel, Torquay;
architect, Dawes Dingle, Torquay.)*

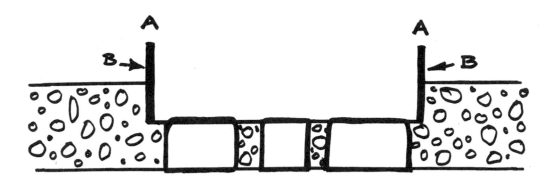

on pieces (slightly smaller than the glass) of polystyrene sheet and cast concrete around these. The polystyrene can be removed after the panel is released.

Combinations of flat panels of slab glasses set in concrete sections of the same thickness can be integrated with thicker concrete sections by placing retaining walls of greased wood, metal or cardboard around the glass panel area before adding the deeper section.

Experiments should be made with small samples to find the texture and consistency of concrete that is most suitable for the particular application.

Figure 15
Simple method of making slab glass set in panel of varying thickness.
A Cardboard, metal or wood retaining walls.
B Greased edges for easy releasing from concrete.

Plate 30
Processes with panels set in concrete.
(a) and (b) Cleaning up panels already set in wooden frame.
(c) Unbolting framework.
(d) Carefully knocking away the frame.
(e) Removing centre piece which divides the panel sections, three panels being cast in the same framework.
(Concrete frames constructed by Maurice Gaye of Hugh Mills and Gaye, Newton Abbot.)

Plates 31 and 32
Details of architectural panel,
14' high, in slab glasses and clear
resins, with metal framework
integrated as part of the design.

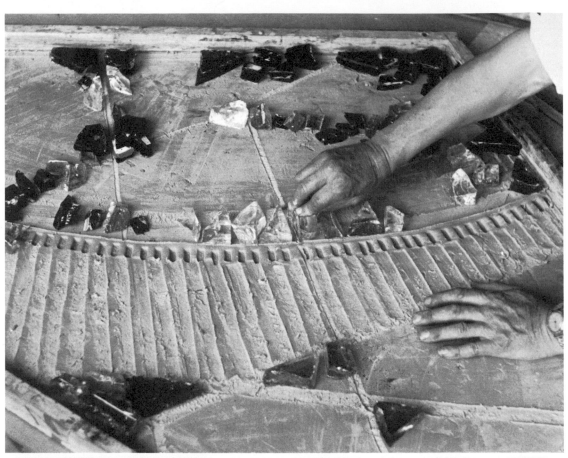

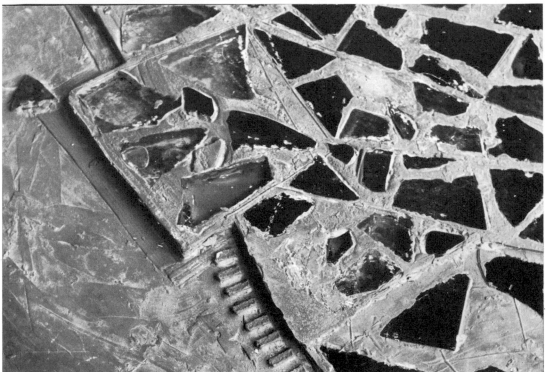

Plate 33
Lawrence Lee has developed an interesting technique whereby glass pieces are placed on a Plasticine reverse mould and the resin mix is poured around it. When cured, the panel is removed and has taken up the surface texture. The photographs show details of the making of a mural for the Convent of the Sacred Heart, Leeds.
(By courtesy of Lawrence Lee and the Oxford University Press.)

Concrete – Concrete is a mixture of cement, aggregate and water. The aggregate is sand and stone chippings of variously graded sizes. A mixture of cement and sand only will give mortar. The quality of the basic material will vary according to the proportions of the ingredients and also the size of the chippings. Aggregate should be evenly graded and must be clean and free from dust. If it is dusty it must be washed well before using and the fine particles washed or sieved out from the chippings. Generally, an average concrete mix is made up of 1 part of cement to 3 parts of aggregate which is first mixed up in the dry state, the water being added a little at a time until the required consistency is obtained. The water used should be clean.

Ordinary builders' cement can be used to make the concrete but Ciment Fondu will be very worthwhile as it is obtainable in both black and white, can be rapid hardening and gives good surface qualities. 'Secar 250' a white refractory ciment fondu, is a good material which is well worth experimenting with to make white or light coloured concretes. Glass fibre mat can be used to strengthen a ciment fondu panel. This will also reduce the weight.

Glass in Filled Resins. The use of concrete is being generally replaced by the use of polyester or epoxy resins mixed with fillers to make up a strong panel which can be made thinner and lighter than concrete. Dry sand or commercial filler powders can be added to the resin to make a mix which can be used around the glass pieces to bond them into the panel form. Design considerations can be varied by the fact that a panel as thin as $\frac{1}{2}$" can be made, allowing the remaining thickness of the 1" glass slab to stand above the surface of the surrounding material. This can give a greater degree of light refraction sparkle to the glass pieces, especially when the edges are chipped to produce facets which will catch the light.

Plate 34 (opposite)
Glass and resin form with irregular
edges, cast in polythene sheeting
with edges raised on wood blocks
but no made mould. The internal
steel frame has become invisible.

Plate 35 (above)
The completed construction (pp.
76–80) in its fixed position in the
entrance hall at National
Westminster Office Buildings,

Draper's Gardens, Throgmorton
Street, London, E.C.2. The
construction is suspended off
the wall by the back support frame
rods.

This design won first prize in a
competition held by the
Worshipful Company of Glaziers
to mark the 8th International
Congress on Glass, held in London
in 1968.

Larger panels will again need strengthening bars bedded in the resin/sand mix.

Where any amount of mixing is to take place, of concrete or resin with fillers, mechanical methods will be of great use. Small mixers can be bought or made up by making a rotating drum driven by an electric motor. A fixed arm will mix the material as the drum rotates.

Figure 16
Thin panel made from resin and filler powder – sand etc.

In experimental work, especially in schools, where quick results are required as cheaply as possible. there is no reason why glass panels should not be made up using plaster as the bonding material. Interior screens or panels can be made up quickly and inexpensively and could be fairly permanent in suitable applications, while having the advantages of being able to be broken up and the glass recovered for other uses, without too much trouble. Dental plaster can be used. This is inexpensive, but in more permanent applications it is worth while making use of 'Herculite' plaster, which although more costly, is stronger and expands less than the dental type when setting. It should be noted that plaster expands slightly on setting, unlike unfilled resins, which usually contract as they harden. See photos in Plate 36, a–f.

Plate 36
A panel created by beginners at school. More sophisticated designs can of course be carried out once the technique has been mastered.
(a) and (b) The frame is lightly stuck down to the glass with Cow Gum.
(c) 'Cubes' of slab glass chopped on the anvil with a tungsten-tipped hammer are placed into the frame and stuck down lightly with Cow Gum.
(d) Pouring in plaster. Plaster-strengthening additives can be mixed in.
(e) The hardened panel is turned over and the glass at the back gently eased off and removed.
(f) Cleaning up edges. Frame may be removed or left in position – if to be removed, sides should have been greased in advance.

(a)

(b)

(c)

(d)

(e)

(f)

Plate 37
Glass, resin and metal
construction by the author.

Plate 38 (opposite)
Free-standing form with slab
glasses embedded into a mortar
of builder's sand and Araldite,
the metal bars being embedded
with the glass. Surface texture
and modelling can be built up
with tools in this technique.

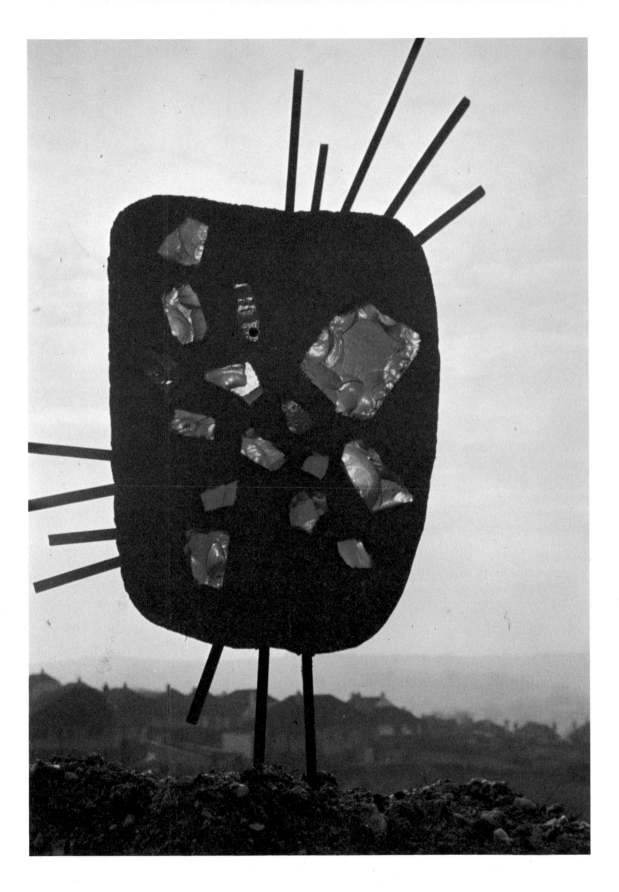

GLASS APPLIQUE

Coloured or clear pieces of sheet or antique glass
can be bonded to a base panel of sheet or plate glass
with epoxy resin. Where deeper tones are used, the
straight forward amber toned epoxy can be used but
if maximum clarity is essential, the 'water white' resin
should be obtained. Polyester resin is not suitable
for use in bonding thin glasses other than in
temporary jobs or experimental sketches, as they
will de-laminate in time. Even with epoxy resins
great care must be taken to ensure that all the glass
used is absolutely clean and free from grease,
otherwise pieces will de-laminate in time causing
pieces to come away from the backing sheet. Where
this process is to be used to glaze exterior windows
a double glazing system should be used so that the
sheet with the decorative elements is not exposed
directly to the open air or subject to condensation,
otherwise the same problem may arise. Large sheets
of glass expand and contract quite considerably
when exposed to direct sunlight and varying
temperatures and for this reason a slightly flexible
epoxy may be found to be more suitable.

In spite of these difficulties, glass appliqué is an
exciting medium in which to work and the basic
techniques can be extended in various ways to
produce work of great beauty and interest.

The technique is open to considerable variation of
treatment. After the sheet or antique glasses which
form the design are cut and have been stuck onto
the base glass, placed over a sketch cartoon if
necessary, the areas or gaps between the glasses can
be filled by brushing in black or coloured opaque
pigment. This will give the treated area a totally
different appearance by containing each piece of
glass by a dark line or area.

Experiments should be carried out to find out whether a particular design or treatment needs this opaque grouting over part or all of the areas decorated. The application of the opaque pigment should be carried out when the glass pieces are firmly bonded by the hardened resin onto the base glass.

Experimental work using several (two or more) sheets of glass appliqué in depth is worth pursuing, as rich and exciting work can result. The greater the depth between the sheet glasses the greater will be the visual movement between the design elements on each glass to the viewer as he moves in relation to the work. Screens can be very effective in this technique, especially when edge lighting can be built in to the design.

It is basically a very simple method of using glass and it can of course be used in conjunction with the glass and metal technique described in the previous section of this book.

GLASS MOSAIC

Mosaic panels can be made up quite simply using smaller off cuts from glasses used in other jobs. Once any work is undertaken in coloured glass it is remarkable how soon a mass of off cuts and chippings accumulate and, as mentioned already, it is worthwhile keeping boxes for waste from each type of glass. Even the smallest pieces will come in useful in another job. The fact that this material is readily at hand will also generate ideas as to how it can be used in new work, and mosaic panels are an ideal application. The principle is simple and generally well known, but again may be varied to give different effects. Two basic methods can be used to give either completely flush surfaced panels, or textured panels with irregular surfaces.

Plate 39
Panel in glass and resin set in a
steel frame which becomes part of
the design. Black grouting of
pigmented, filled resin has been
used around some of the glass
pieces. By the author.

Plate 40 (opposite)
Standing construction 2' 6" high
in slab glass and resin mortar on a
steel frame. By the author. The
stem is supported in a stone block
base.

H

A smooth, flush surface can be made by sticking cut
rectangles, or irregular pieces, of coloured sheet,
antique or slab glass face down, on their flat side,
onto a strong piece of brown paper. The composition
can be built up freely, or a formal design can be
worked out and drawn onto the paper first, bearing
in mind that you are working in reverse from the
back of the panel. Each piece of glass should be
stuck to the paper by a light adhesive – strong
enough to hold the pieces onto the sheet, but easily
removable from the front of the panel once it has
been cast. Cow Gum, a rubber solution or ordinary
paste mixed from household flour and water will be
satisfactory for this.

A retaining frame should be made up to hold in the
casting material, which can be plaster, ciment fondu
or filled and pigmented polyester or epoxy resin.
Frames similar to those described in the Glass and
Resin Section will be satisfactory. This framework
could be left as a permanent edge finish and could
be made up from aluminium or other metal strip or
angle section. The best colour for the casting
material will usually be white (Secar white
refactory ciment is excellent) to give the glass
colour a greater chance to show up, but other
colours may be added, if needed. A permanent
framework is desirable in larger panels, otherwise
strengthening bars and hessian in plaster or glass
fibre mat in resin should be bonded in to give
strength. A highly polished finish can be obtained by
casting face down onto a glass sheet, as described
in the Section on Glass and Concrete. If a polyester
or epoxy mix is used a releasing wax should be
polished onto the glass sheet. The panel is removed
from the sheet as described in that Section. If a
permanent frame is wanted it should be stuck down
onto the glass sheet with Cow Gum. The glass sheet
must be placed on a flat surface so that no gaps
occur between the frame and glass. The gum will

seat the frame down long enough for the casting operation.

The completed cast panel should be cleaned up when the casting surface has been removed. This treatment is good for applications such as table tops where flat surfaces are essential.

Plate 41 (opposite)
Detail of glass and concrete panel.
By the author.

Plate 42
'Bat form' – sculpture with steel
and slab glass.
By the author.

6
WORKSHOP LAYOUT

The size of work to be undertaken will obviously determine the working area required. Smaller pieces can be readily made in a temporary working area, using existing tables or benches covered with hardboard sheeting for glass work and polythene when resins are being used. Metalwork can be made up using existing workshop facilities where they are available. Small amounts of resins are easily stored in screw top tins in a cupboard which should not have a temperature of more than about 60°F (15°C). Great care must always be taken where polyesters are concerned to see that the catalyst (hardener), which is usually an organic peroxide and the accelerator (cobalt soap) are kept apart to avoid accidental direct mixing together (this can lead to spontaneous combustion). They should also be kept off absorbent surfaces which may become saturated with either liquid. If they have to be placed on wooden shelving – line the surface with glass or polythene sheeting. An ideal storage method for organic peroxide is to make a 'safe' from concrete blocks, with a concrete floor. A separate one should be used for accelerators.

Larger amounts of materials should lead to careful organization of storage space. An area must be allowed for the pouring, weighing and mixing of resins near to the resin storage area. Glass cutting and shaping should be situated in another area with the glass stock near at hand.

Some amount of layout method and organization will always be repaid in the saving of time searching for tools etc. Where more than one person is working over a period of time, cleaning up should be undertaken willingly and methodically to avoid confusion which can lead to wasted work. Where school work is being undertaken the teacher will have to see that each stage of a job is well prepared for and that the conditions are suitable for the production of work. It should be possible to allow senior students the opportunity of making exciting experimental work without causing too much upheaval in the Craft Room, but adequate preparation time should be given to projects so that all aspects of work — (materials required — elementary precautions — methods of working with materials etc.) are understood.

The methods and materials described in this book are essentially flexible in use. This fact does mean that it is difficult to lay down hard and fast rules as to exact workshop layout. Once the material areas are allocated the actual working areas should be as simple and as flexible as can be allowed as each job can vary enormously in scale and design. I find that instead of benches, sheets of blockboard 2' 6" wide and 6' long held firm by stout timber joists running lengthwise along the under edges and supported by empty 56 lb resin drums make good adaptable layout benches for all types of work. Wider areas can be built up by placing two of these side by side — one board can be placed on top of another for additional height. The whole thing can be cleared away easily when the maximum floor space is needed.

The best floor surface for a glass/resin workshop is concrete as it will have to stand up to hard wear and messy materials. Wet resin spills are best coped with by sprinkling with sand, which will soak it up and make cleaning easier. Hardened resin droppings will have to be either left, or chipped off with a hammer when hard.

Plate 43 (opposite)
Window in leaded glass and glass
mosaic in three layers, by Keith
New. In the chapel of the Church
Missionary Society, Waterloo
Road, London, S.E.1.

Plate 44
Glass in concrete window at St
Edmund's, Hayes. By Lawrence
Lee.

APPENDIX
MATERIAL SUPPLIERS

GLASS

Slab and Antique Glasses
James Hetley & Co. Ltd.,
Beresford Avenue, Wembley, Middlesex.
(English slabs and antiques).

T. & W. Ide Ltd.,
Glasshouse Fields, Cable Street, London, E.1.
Tel. 01-790 2333.
(French slabs of St Just-sur-Loire Glass Factory).

**Float – Plate – Sheet – Wired and
Textured Glass**
Any good local glass merchant.

POLYESTER RESINS

For bulk orders:
B.I.P. Chemicals Ltd.,
Popes Lane, Oldbury, P.O. Box 6, Warley, Worcs.
Tel. 021-552 1551.
Clear resin – 800
Clear resin with wax – 856
Flexible resin – 4134

Scott Bader Ltd.,
Wollaston, Wellingborough, Northamptonshire.
Tel. Wellingborough 4881.
Clear resin – 191 E – low viscosity (thin)
Clear resin – 191 M.V. – medium viscosity (thicker)
Clear resin – 306. Fire retardant
Flexible resin – 182
Accelerator W – (with wax additive for surface tack).

For small orders of 1 lb upwards:-
Scott Bader Suppliers:
1. Trylon Ltd.,
   Thrift Street, Wollaston.
   Tel. Wollaston 275.

2. Automobile Plastics Ltd.,
   Autoplay House, 7 Henry Road, New Barnet, Herts.
   Tel. 01-449 9147.
3. Bartoline (Hull) Ltd.,
   Swinemoor Industries Estate, Beverley, Yorks.
   Tel. Beverley 882185.
4. James Coates Bros. Ltd.,
   1 Townley St., Middleton, Manchester.
   Tel. 061-643 2653.
5. Strand Glass Co. Ltd.,
   79 High St., Brentford, Middlesex.
   Tel. 01-560 0978.
6. R. C. Laker,
   67 Kiln Road, Wokingham, Berks.

CATALYST AND ACCELERATOR

Novadel Ltd.,
St. Anns Crescent, Wandsworth, London, S.W.18.

Alec Tiranti Ltd.,
72 Charlotte St., London, W.1.

Resin suppliers also supply these to match their
own products.

EPOXY RESINS

Emerson & Cuming (U.K.) Ltd.,
Colville Road, Acton, London, W.3.
Tel. 01-992 6692.

Emerson & Cuming, Inc.,
Canton, Massachusetts.
Clear Epoxy Resin — Stycast 1264 (2-part)

CIBA (A.R.L.) Ltd.,
Duxford, Cambridge.
Tel. Sawston 2121.
Clear Epoxy Resin — MY 790
Hardener — X83/319
Flexibiliser — DY 040

Plate 45
Glass and steel construction by
the author.

'Araldite' Epoxy (Golden Yellow) MY 750 and
MY 753 and Hardener HY 951 or HY 956
'Araldite' Colouring Pastes for Epoxy (opaque)

Translucent Dyes for Epoxy
CIBA, Clayton Ltd.,
Clayton, Manchester, 11.

ACRYLIC

Tensol No. 7. 2-part mix

I.C.I. Plastics Division
Welwyn Garden City, Herts.
(Also sales offices in Bristol,
Birmingham, Manchester,
Glasgow and Belfast).

Acrifix 90. 2-part mix
Tensol No. 7. 2-part mix

Röhm & Haas GmbH
6100 Darmstadt, Western Germany.

Supplied in UK by
Cornelius Chemical Co. Ltd.,
Ibex House,
Minories, London, E.C.3.

RESINS AND EQUIPMENT

Alec Tiranti,
72 Charlotte Street, London, W.1.
Suppliers of resins and most materials required to
work with them. Personal shoppers welcomed.
Resins. Pigments. Catalysts and Accelerators. Brushes
and Tools. Barrier Creams etc. Technical Books.

EQUIPMENT

Downland Equipment,
K & C Mouldings (England) Ltd.,
Spa House, Shelfanger, Diss, Norfolk.
Tel. Diss 2660.
Scales. Measuring Dispensers. Brushes. Rollers.
Masks. Respirators and Protective Equipment and
other items.

GLASS FIBRE

For bulk orders
Fibreglass Ltd., Reinforcements Division,
Valley Road, Birkenhead.

Smaller amounts

Alec Tiranti Ltd.

Scott Bader stockists.

COLOUR PASTES AND PIGMENTS

Alec Tiranti Ltd.

Llewellyn Ryland Ltd., Balsall Heath Works,
Haden Street, Birmingham, 12.
Tel. 021-440 2284.

CELLULOSE FILM

British Cellophane Ltd.,
9 Henrietta Place, London, W.1.
Tel. 01-636 8311.

British Sidac Ltd.,
Hesketh House, Portman Square, London, W.1.
Tel. 01-935 4463.

POLYTHENE SHEETING

From local builders' merchants.

FILLERS AND REINFORCEMENTS

Alec Tiranti Ltd.

Croxton and Garry Ltd.,
Windsor House, Esher, Surrey (bulk supplies).

FLEXIBLE MOULD MATERIALS

Silicone Rubber
Midland Silicones Ltd.,
68 Knightsbridge, London, S.W.1.

I.C.I. Ltd.,
I.C.I. House, Millbank, London, S.W.1.

Alec Tiranti Ltd.

Vinyl Hot Melt
Vinatex Ltd.,
Devonshire House, Carshalton, Surrey.

Alec Tiranti Ltd.

RELEASE AGENTS

Alec Tiranti Ltd.

Downland,
K. & C. Mouldings (England) Ltd.

POLYESTER 'MORTAR'

'ISOPON' 2-part mix (resin and hardener)
'CATALOY' 2-part mix (resin and hardener)
'TETROSYL' 2-part mix (resin and hardener)
obtainable in 14 or 16 lb cans from shops and
factors selling car body fillers.

INDEX